LEGENDS OF THE DALLAS COWBOYS

LEGENDS OF THE DALLAS COWBOYS

TOM LANDRY, TROY AIKMAN, EMMITT SMITH,
AND OTHER COWBOYS STARS

CODY MONK

SPORTS
PUBLISHING

Sports Publishing books may be purchased in bulk at special discounts for sales promotion, corporate gifts, fund-raising, or educational purposes. Special editions can also be created to specifications. For details, contact the Special Sales Department, Sports Publishing, 307 West 36th Street, 11th Floor, New York, NY 10018 or sportspubbooks@skyhorsepublishing.com.

Sports Publishing® is a registered trademark of Skyhorse Publishing, Inc.®, a Delaware corporation.

Visit our website at www.sportspubbooks.com

10 9 8 7 6 5 4 3 2 1

Library of Congress Cataloging-in-Publication Data is available on file.

Cover design by Tom Lau
Cover photo credit Associated Press

ISBN: 978-1-68358-137-6
Ebook ISBN: 978-1-68358-154-3

Printed in the United States of America

*To Courtney, Alexis, Keelin Grace
and Berkeley: thank you.*

CONTENTS

PREFACE

On fall Sunday mornings in West Texas, even the preacher kept a close eye on his watch. If services at First Baptist Church of Farwell, Texas, went much past 11:45 a.m., the focus among parishioners turned from defeating Satan to defeating the Redskins or Giants, who, in that part of the world, are considered one with Lucifer.

The smart preachers in the area knew how to work around Cowboys games. The offering plate was always passed early in the service, just in case some folks slid out after the singing to catch *The NFL Today* before the noon kickoff. If Dallas had the late game, the preacher made sure to give an especially good effort in the morning because his second chance during the 6 p.m. service would be in front of friends and family.

In my hometown 90 miles northwest of Lubbock, the football week is a pyramid of competition starting on Thursday night. It begins with the junior high and junior varsity high school games, where schools get a look at future prospects and those on the JV get a chance to show why they should be playing the next day. Friday nights are special in Texas. The intra-school competition that existed the night before now has become one small town against another.

On Saturdays, folks from all over those small towns jam college stadiums from Lubbock to Austin to College Station to tighten up the pyramid even more. They may have been trying to knock each other into the next county the night before, but, on Saturdays, they are united as Red Raiders and Longhorns and Aggies against Bears and Mustangs and Horned Frogs.

Sunday, though, is the most sacred of football days. That is, unless Dallas is playing on Monday night. On Cowboys game day, any collegiate loyalty is put aside for the greater good of the state and the nation of Cowboy. It's the only day where something is more important in the state than oil and cattle prices or a Neiman Marcus sale.

Farwell borders the Texas-New Mexico state line and is about equidistant from Denver and Dallas. However, for me, Broncos games were either something to watch after the Cowboys or something to discuss during commercials.

My Cowboys loyalty came naturally. On my earliest visits to my grandparents, my uncle Kelly Jo would make sure I was in front of the television to watch Tony Dorsett and Drew Pearson and Randy White. My mother fed the fire with the famous poster of the Doomsday Defense posing in a graveyard with headstones reading New York, Washington, Pittsburgh, etc. I put the poster on my ceiling and drifted to sleep with dreams of devouring quarterbacks like "Too Tall" Jones, John Dutton, and Harvey Martin.

I was Danny White in the backyard, with buddies playing the roles of Dorsett and Ron Springs behind me and Pearson and Tony Hill on the outside. I defended passes using names like Everson Walls, Michael Downs, and Ron Fellows. And when I did, I had Todd, the older kid that was always around, scribble stars on my replica Cowboys helmet, always followed by "Coach Landry says, 'Good job today, son.'" Then, I went inside and tried to work Herschel Walker-like trades to get the most Cowboys football cards. Cowboys fever so struck me that I was even nice to my sister when she demanded television control to watch *Dallas*. I didn't know J.R. Ewing from Patrick Ewing. All I wanted to see was the aerial shot of the hole in Texas Stadium in the program's opener.

As I got older, Sundays became more difficult. By the time I got to junior high, I sat with the cool kids on the right side of church. More than once I snuck out of the service and to the car to catch Brad Sham and Dale Hansen's pregame show on the Cowboys Radio Network. More than one time my mother scolded my decision. More than one time my dad wanted to know if Brad and Dale had anything interesting to say.

When it came to Sunday lunch, Mom and Dad took a united stance. No TV until the plate was cleared. That was quickly circumvented as I would take just enough for Mom not to complain. On gamedays, even hunger took a back seat.

Monday night Cowboys games were special. My dad wasn't a huge fan, but he enjoyed the games because he knew they meant so much to me. Those Mondays were the only nights I was allowed to stay up past 10 p.m. In addition to it being a Dallas game, those nights were special because I got to hear former Cowboys great Don Meredith and Howard Cosell on the call. I also knew it was at least three hours I would get with my dad. Even though he had a whole work week staring him in the face, he sat there attentively every Monday night. My living and dying on every play was probably just as entertaining for him as the game. I would watch the game like I was the show's stats guy. I took notes feverishly and compiled my own statistics. In a time before the Internet and the specialized statistic, my homemade stats were probably just as good as the actual crew's.

Into high school and college, the names and the fortunes changed. Jerry Jones bought the team, replaced Landry and Tex Schramm, and brought in an influx of new talent. It didn't matter because I rooted for the logo. Quickly, the names of Aikman, Irvin, and Emmitt became beloved. Another Trinity to believe in for this Panhandle boy.

It is in this Cowboys fan's view that I wrote *Legends of the Dallas Cowboys*. Choosing the chapters was agonizing. Because I saw some play only on old NFL Films shows, giving the book a more current look was tempting. But, the Cowboys were built by the Bob Lillys, Mel Renfros, Lee Roy Jordans, Merediths, and Bob Hayeses. The organization is "America's Team" because of Landry's fedora and Tex Schramm's innovation. There are familiar stories, some not-so-familiar ones, and those that went on to become legends. It is a look at the team and its legacy through a fan that has a lifelong history with the team.

Part of that history is a recent one that has led to a unique niche for this book. When I started covering the Cowboys for *The Dallas Morning News* Spanish-language newspaper, *Al Día,* I got a different look at the team. I saw just how much of an impact "America's Team" has south of the border. In Mexico, people in the Baja, south of San Diego, root for the Oakland Raiders. The rest of the country is blanketed by the blue and silver star. The Cowboys have season ticket holders that travel to Texas Stadium from Mexico City, Monterrey, Guadalajara, and other Mexican cities.

From the depths of Mexico to small town Texas pulpits and Everytown, USA, the reach of "America's team" does encompass all.

—Cody Monk
June 4, 2004

INTRODUCTION

The 2016 Dallas Cowboys season brought surprise and dreaded familiarity. While the team likely found its newest franchise quarterback in Dak Prescott and workhorse running back in Ezekiel Elliott and finished with the NFC's best record, the Cowboys still couldn't win a playoff game, losing 34–31 at home to Green Bay in the Divisional Round. It was another maddening loss for a storied organization that has only three playoff wins since the last Super Bowl victory in 1996.

As the fourth pick in the 2016 NFL Draft, Elliott's rise was expected. What the Cowboys didn't anticipate was a fourth-round pick (No. 135 overall) shining in the preseason and, ultimately, unseating long-time fixture Tony Romo under center. The Cowboys are clearly Prescott's and Elliott's. Romo is now a broadcaster and trying to qualify for golf's U.S. Open. The offensive line is one of the best in football (three 2017 Pro Bowl selections), anchored by All-Pro guard Zack Martin, the guy the Cowboys chose in the 2014 NFL Draft instead of Johnny Manziel. The defense is aggressive and compliments the methodical process coach Jason Garrett likes to follow in all facets, but especially on offense.

With Romo retired, Prescott firmly entrenched, and Garrett giving the coaching position much-needed stability, the Cowboys are entering a new era.

With fans looking forward, this version of Legends of the Dallas Cowboys looks both to the team's storied past and its present. Newly included are chapters on offensive lineman Larry Allen and Owner/General Manager Jerry Jones.

Allen was beloved during his 12 seasons in Dallas. Strong, imposing, and dominating, the man who once bench pressed 700 pounds and is considered one of the best offensive lineman to ever play, Allen is in both the Cowboys' Ring of Honor and the Pro Football Hall of Fame. This chapter looks at his humble beginnings in Compton, California, up to the day he was inducted in Canton.

Joining Allen soon in Canton will be Jerry Jones, a member of the 2017 Pro Football Hall of Fame class. Widely respected as an owner, Cowboys fans gristle at Jerry Jones the General Manager. And, though Jones was named the NFL's "Executive of the Year" in 2014, the misses have far outweighed the hits for this part of Jones's job description. This chapter looks at what fuels Jones and his long-time quest for another Super Bowl.

With two new stars to go with established ones in Jason Witten, Dez Bryant, and Sean Lee and a franchise that is the world's most valuable sports platform, the Dallas Cowboys continue to dominate league business and television ratings. Five of the NFL's six highest-rated 2016 games involved Dallas. The 2016 Cowboys-Redskins Thanksgiving game was the most-watched game in Fox history and the most-watched regular season game since Dallas-Kansas City in 1995.

So, business off-the-field continues to be good and is looking better between the lines. The next step, for the franchise and its dedicated fan base, is shedding that familiar, unpleasant feeling that has become a January staple.

—Cody Monk
May 5, 2017

ACKNOWLEDGMENTS

Thanks to Skyhorse Publishing and Julie Ganz for keeping the "Legends" series going. Special thanks to Mike Burdick, Ted Gangi, Barton Jenkins, Dan Kelly, Augustin Lopez, Sarah McPhillips, Alexander Morales, Francisco Ng, Ben Perez-Martinez, Andres Quintero, Mario Rentería, Tricia Sibley, Reinaldo Suarez, and Sara Voyard.

LEGENDS OF THE DALLAS COWBOYS

TOM LANDRY

I t was a day all too Pittsburgh, the kind of gray fall afternoon that defines the blue-collar town. The wind was blowing so hard off the river that Pitt Stadium became a sea of garbage and piercing breezes: an ideal setting for the hard-nosed Pittsburgh Steelers.

It was 1965, the halfway point in Tom Landry's sixth season as head coach of the Dallas Cowboys. Two years previous, owner Clint Murchison, wanting to establish consistency for the expansion franchise, gave Landry a 10-year extension, despite Landry having won only 13 of his first 54 games. Landry was their man. But, their man wasn't producing. On this blustery, cold day in Pittsburgh, all of Landry's fears came calling.

Bob Lilly, Don Meredith, Mel Renfro, Bob Hayes, and Chuck Howley headed a team that had gone 5–8–1 in 1964 for the team's fifth straight fifth place finish in the NFL East. Still, the feeling around the league was that 1965 would be the year the Cowboys made their first NFL impact. Lilly had emerged as one of the most dominant defensive tackles in the league the year before, making his first of 11 straight Pro Bowls. Renfro had done the same in the secondary, making the Pro Bowl squad in 1964 for the first of his 10 consecutive selections. The offense was coming off a year in which it averaged less than 18 points per game. But, Landry felt like Meredith would bounce back and that adding rookie receiver Bob Hayes would give the Cowboys a speed weapon no other NFL team had.

Things looked good the first two weeks after Dallas, at the Cotton Bowl, ran over the New York Giants and Washington. In the season-opening win, 31–2 over the Giants, Meredith hit Hayes twice for 81 yards, including a

TOM LANDRY

Born: September 11, 1924, in Mission, Texas
Died: February 12, 2000, from leukemia
Position: Head Coach
Years with the Cowboys: 1960–1988
Record: 250-162-6
Playoff Records: 20–16
Honors:
* 20 consecutive winning seasons
* 2 Super Bowl titles
* 2 NFL Championship Game appearances
* 13 divisional titles
* 1966 NFL Coach of the Year
* 1975 NFC Coach of the Year
* Third-winningest NFL coach with a 270-178–6 overall record
* Inducted into the Pro Football Hall of Fame in 1990
* Inducted into the Ring of Honor in 1993

45-yard touchdown in the second half in which Hayes took a routine screen pass and went the rest of the way untouched.

After flattening the Redskins 27–7, the Cowboys were 2–0 and the offense was humming. Then came a five-game stretch that put the team on the road three straight weeks and four of five. When the team left Dallas, the offense and the winning stayed behind. The Cowboys lost four straight, putting up only 20 combined points in losses to Cleveland and Green Bay leading up to the Halloween game against the Steelers.

This day was much of the same for Dallas. Meredith was inconsistent, throwing interceptions, fumbling in key situations deep in Pittsburgh territory. The defense allowed Bill Nelson, the Steelers' third stringer, to throw for 272 yards and three touchdowns. Even Hayes and Renfro were bad with Hayes dropping a key third-down pass and Renfro fumbling his second punt in two weeks, which led to a Steelers touchdown. It was an all-unit breakdown that resulted in a monumental postgame breakdown. Landry entered the locker room after the game and asked everyone but the players to give him a few minutes. With nothing but his guys surrounding him, Landry thanked everyone for working hard but said he was disappointed with the way things had gone in his Dallas tenure. He said he thought his time as Cowboys coach was drawing to a close. Then, the stoic man with the never-changing look broke down in tears. "[His crying] really touched us," Lilly said later. "We knew we had to play harder." Playing harder started the next week at the Cotton Bowl with a 39–31 win over San Francisco, followed by a redemption victory over the Steelers the next week at home, 24–17.

It was the last time Dallas would lose to Pittsburgh until the 1976 Super Bowl, a string of seven straight wins.

The Landry breakdown inspired the Cowboys to wins in five of their last seven games. Dallas finished the season 7–7 and made the playoffs.

The next season, the team had its first winning season, the first of 20 straight under Landry. "That game in Pittsburgh,"

> "That game in Pittsburgh was a key point in the organization. It was the turning point for the Cowboys."
>
> [BOB LILLY]

Lilly said, "was a key point in the organization. It was the turning point for the Cowboys."

That tearful day was almost the end for Landry. At the time of the Halloween affair in Pittsburgh, Landry was in the midst of his sixth season. He had won less than 30 percent of his games and felt he had done all he could with what he had. The team was giving the kind of effort he wanted, executing his new, innovative ideas on both sides of the ball and utilizing weapons such as Hayes that had never been used before in the NFL. Still, the team wasn't getting results.

So much so that the man whose fedora is the lasting image of America's most recognized sports team and whose legacy continues to define a city almost wasn't to be. "I don't know what it was," Lilly said. "We gave a little extra after that game. Had we not, he may not have been around."

AP/WWP

ABOVE: Cowboys coach Tom Landry and defensive end Ed "Too Tall" Jones try on helmets borrowed from a couple London "Bobbies" during a practice to prepare to play the Chicago Bears in London during the 1986 preseason.

FRAT DADDY

Tom Landry was never mistaken for the average khakis, white shirt and tie, and blue blazer-wearing frat dude while at the University of Texas. A receding hairline and his status as a war veteran kind of made Landry stand out.

Landry, who came from Mission High School in the Rio Grande Valley, played the 1942 season at UT under Hall of Fame coach D.X. Bible before heading to a B-17 and war-torn Europe. At 19, he was handed his wings and a copilot spot in the Eighth Air Force, based out of England. Landry flew 30 World War II missions, mostly over Czechoslovakia, and survived a crash inside Belgium.

When he returned to Texas, he was in his mid-20s and far more mature than most of his young teammates.

A lot had changed since Landry left. Blair Cherry was in, Bible out. Bobby Layne was in at quarterback, Landry's original position, and Landry's move to defense was imminent. Landry showed his maturity by not complaining about the move. The move from quarterback was a disappointment, but Cherry wanted Landry and Layne on the same field.

Landry was never an All-American. Never even All-Conference. But, he was a vital leader. Against SMU in 1947, he was in the backfield to stop the Mustangs' all-world running back Doak Walker, despite having an injury that forced him to wrap up with only one arm. The Longhorns lost the game 14–13, but playing Landry showed the kind of confidence Cherry had in him. "He had more confidence in Tom with one arm in a cast than some backup with two arms," teammate Pepe Blount said.

Landry was a quiet leader, choosing his words and his timing carefully. He wasn't a drinker, a cusser, or a rebel rouser. But he was far from a church and choir-only guy. He was a member of the wild Cowboys fraternity. As part of his initiation, Landry was stripped nude, decorated with honey and cereal, dropped off outside Austin, and forced to flag down help to get back to campus. The stoic, stone-faced legend stripped and stranded.

TEXAN BECOMES A YANKEE

It only seemed like Tom Landry was in Texas his whole life. He actually cut his NFL teeth in Gotham City. It is still hard for any Cowboys fan to admit the long-despised place produced the most legendary figure in the organization's history.

Landry was in New York 10 years, first as an All-Pro defensive back and then as an unparalleled defensive coach. From 1949 to 1959, Landry helped the Giants emerge from a three-team New York to the most dominant team in the league. So dominant that the Giants knocked the other two teams, the Yankees and the Bulldogs, out of the city and put the Giants at the head of the NFL lineup, replacing the stalwart Cleveland Browns and Los Angeles Rams.

Before Landry became a Giant, though, he was a Yankee. The football team went the way of the eight-track tape after one season because of dollar issues. The way things were then, teams in that territory had rights to the Yankees' players. So, Landry became a default Giant.

The Giants didn't have to retain Landry. They did, Landry was convinced, "because of my punting ability." He became an All-Pro, even though Sam Huff said he couldn't imagine Landry as a player. "Slow, no hair," Huff said. "Exactly what a coach is supposed to look like."

So much so that Landry began his defensive wizardry before his playing days were done. He coined the term *red dog* for blitzes, a term many coaches still use. As a player, Landry came up with the Giants' "Umbrella Secondary." Suddenly, it was Landry and the Giants defense that was stealing the headlines. "On defense, you have to constantly anticipate and react," Landry once said. "On offense, all of the plays are diagramed and designed and the unit knows ahead of time exactly where it's going and what it's going to do. That's why I felt defense was the most challenging part of the game."

With the Giants, Landry went to the NFL title game each of his last three years in New York. He did so alongside an offensive coordinator he would later do major battle with—Vince Lombardi.

Landry played alongside Frank Gifford and had Hall of Famers such as Huff at his disposal. He was even big buddies with budding broadcaster

Howard Cosell, who was Landry's Connecticut commuting compatriot. "I don't really know what it was," Landry said before a game against the Giants, "but those days and those teams had something special about them."

RANGERS BOUND

When Landry first came to Dallas, he didn't even have a team to coach. He was also going to be working for general manager Tex Schramm, a man that had general manager experience but had been hired away from a TV network. Although there is no lack of sports media people who think they could do it nowadays, making the leap from media to running a new team was novel. And, Landry was taking a huge risk, leaving his job as New York Giants defensive coordinator to work alongside this media guy.

Landry knew very little about what he was getting into when he accepted the Dallas job in late 1959. No one else did, either. On January 28, 1960, in Miami Beach, Florida, the NFL awarded Clint Murchison and Bedford Wynn the league's 13th team. Perhaps it was fitting that Landry was already in place when the group got the team because the day was also Landry's 11th wedding anniversary. "Guess this is the day that great things happen for me," Landry told the *Dallas Morning News* that day. And for the Dallas . . . Rangers?

Even before the NFL approved Murchison's and Wynn's bid, the group decided they wanted the name to be the Rangers. It eventually was changed to the Cowboys to avoid confusion with a local baseball team that eventually folded. However, the famous headline appeared in Dallas papers in December 1959 proclaiming "Rangers Hire Landry."

Getting Landry had as much to do with location as it did with the opportunity. Landry, a native of Mission, Texas, and his UT sweetheart, Alicia, wanted to get back to Texas. Both had family in the Dallas area, but Landry first had to decide which Texas city he wanted to call home.

> **"Guess this is the day that great things happen for me."**
>
> [TOM LANDRY]

In those days, football folks had to work in the off season. The game simply didn't pay well enough to support a wife and four kids. So, in between inventing the Flex defense, which led to the modern-day 4–3 and the shotgun formation that led to the wide-open offense that the NFL enjoys, Landry peddled insurance policies. He was especially big in the oil and gas business and the new kids from the new team in the new league in Houston tried to take advantage of Landry's off-season gig.

The Oilers, playing in the fledgling American Football League, and their owner, big-time oil man Bud Adams, offered Landry the head coaching job. Adams also offered Landry all of the insurance business at Adams's petroleum companies, worth, according to reports, around $65,000, a righteous amount in those days. Adams was also offering a bigger salary than the Dallas team and the opportunity to coach Heisman Trophy winner Billy Cannon.

But, something didn't sit right with Landry. The AFL was throwing around the bucks, but the NFL was the bigger name. It had the stability, and

AP/WWP

Landry's innovative nature and defensive reputation had already given him an enormously high profile, bigger than some head coaches.

Landry chose the stability of the NFL and the uncertainty of the Cowboys. The team would be stocked with players from other teams and, because the Cowboys were admitted too late to take part in the 1960 draft, college free agents. They would also play as a "swing" team. They would play every other team in the now 13-team league and be admitted to a division once Minnesota came on board the following season.

Because Landry knew a lot of people around the league, he began making calls, begging owners to help him out. "I made a real plea to the NFL owners that we were going into Dallas, fighting another league and we needed players," Landry told the *Dallas Morning News* "I was at my best. They said, 'We'll help you.'"

The expansion draft wasn't much different than what it is today. Clubs protected all but eight players on their roster, and a team could lose as many as three players. When one player was picked, the team got to protect another of the original eight.

Knowing they wouldn't be formed in time for the draft, the front office signed more than 30 players to "personal services" contracts before the NFL team handed them the reigns to a team. It was a mixture of formality (that the NFL would give them the team) and brashness by Schramm and Landry. Landry admitted at the time, "I don't really know [our players]." Among those Landry didn't know was SMU quarterback Don Meredith and New Mexico running back Don Perkins. "We won't have a championship team," Landry said the day after the franchise was announced. "But, I think we'll have a good one. We'll have 36 players with professional experience, and that is something."

That something was an 0–11–1 season, the only time the team has ever gone winless. "I hate to say it, but those [early] teams were awful because that's a discredit to those guys," Landry told the *Dallas Morning News* in a 1989 interview. "But, we were weak. The worst thing I ever did [in those years] was

LEFT: Landry is carried off the field after winning Super Bowl VI against the Miami Dolphins.

talk [quarterback] Eddie [LaBaron] out of being a lawyer in Midland. We just didn't have enough personnel." At least not yet.

INNOVATION FROM AN INNOVATOR

Landry didn't set out to create the next "gotta have" defense or the latest offensive set. He was just trying to earn his keep and figure out a way to beat Paul Brown's Cleveland Browns teams. As a cornerback for the New York Giants, Landry was making $12,000 to turn in an All-Pro performance and to coach the defense. After one season, Landry walked into Wellington Mara's office and had a sitdown with the Giants owner. Mara's defensive coordinator/left cornerback laid out his accomplishments and asked for a raise. Mara processed the information, leaned back in his chair, and asked Landry if he really thought he deserved a raise. "I just don't know if you've had a good enough year," Mara said with a smile. Landry got his raise, and the Giants kept the man that created the modern 4–3 and Flex defenses, made the shotgun formation the cool thing to do, was always on the forefront of NFL trends, and invented spots for coaches that had never existed previously.

In the mid-1950s, Otto Graham and the Cleveland Browns were ruling the league with Paul Brown's spread offense that allowed Graham more time in the pocket. That led to the receivers being involved more in the play, be it catching passes or blocking for Graham, who was also a solid runner.

Landry figured if he could lessen the number of players needed to contain the base plays up front where the more sophisticated plays began, he could free up more players to pursue the ball. He had his defense line up with six linemen and a linebacker, but at the line of scrimmage two of the linemen would drop back into the linebacker spots. "[With the formation] we shut the Browns down cold," former Giants defensive tackle Al DeRogatis told the *Sporting News*. "Tom was a master technician."

The technician led the Giants to three NFL title games from 1956 to 1959. He had talent, such as linebacker Sam Huff, who says Landry built the modern 4–3 around him. "All of what Landry did led to the zones and man-to-man variances that you see today."

When Landry got to Dallas, he didn't have an All-Pro like Huff. He needed to lessen the burden on his roster of veteran spares and young may-never-bes. In those days, Vince Lombardi's Green Bay Packers were busy try-ing to create a seal here and run the play through the alley. Those alleys were opened by smaller, quicker linemen. Landry figured he could stop the seals from ever forming if the leaner guards and tackles were lying on their backs instead of blocking. He wanted his teams to be able to cut the feet out from any play using only a handful of guys. The rest, he figured, would be freed up to pursue the ball and close off gaps.

In the Flex, the right end and left tackle were nose to nose with offensive linemen, but the left end and right tackle lined up a bit behind the line of scrim-mage to get a better read and more time to find out where the play was headed. As Landry slowly started integrating All-Pros into the formation, the Cowboys became defense dominant. The unit, with Lilly, Lee Roy Jordan, Dave Edwards, Jethro Pugh, George Andrie, and Larry Cole, became the Doomsday Defense, and Dallas became NFL legit.

> "We won't have a championship team. But, I think we'll have a good one. We'll have 36 players with professional experience, and that is something."
>
> [TOM LANDRY]

Getting a guy such as Pugh was also a Landry specialty. The Cowboys snatched up the six-foot-seven Pugh out of Elizabeth City State in North Carolina in the 11th round of the 1965 draft. In those days, guys such as Alex Karras and the bigger, shorter linemen were ruling the NFL line roost. Landry figured with Pugh's height and lean body (260 pounds) he could take longer steps and cover more ground, getting to the quar-terback quicker. Landry did the same years later with another small college player, Ed "Too Tall" Jones of Tennessee State, who looked more suited to take on Karl Malone than Franco Harris.

Landry didn't mind taking chances on the smaller players from smaller programs for two reasons. One, he trusted Schramm and uber-scout Gil Brandt, who got to know every roadside diner from Dallas to Dover, to find him personnel. Secondly, Landry and the Cowboys were the first team to bring in a true strength coach. Landry wanted guys he could mold, and Brandt found them. Once the players got to Dallas, weightlifter Alvin Roy showed them how to properly lift, and Boots Garland, a former college track coach, made sure each player maximized his speed ability. These were the days when players and coaches worked in the off season, and training camp was just that: the place players came to get into shape. That wouldn't be the Cowboy's mantra. Garland and Roy designed programs to maximize potential, and another new position, Ermal Allen and his quality control spot, made sure Dallas was more prepared than other teams. Allen broke down game films and made notes about what

ABOVE: Landry responds to questions after being fired by Jerry Jones, the Cowboys' new owner.

teams were doing in certain situations. When it came to game time, little surprised Landry's boys. "Tom was always playing cat and mouse with his own formations," Huff said. "He'd come up with some kind of new offense and then immediately create a defense to stop it."

Landry's biggest offensive innovation wasn't anything the league hadn't seen before. It was just something no one had dusted off for a while. The 49ers had used the shotgun formation when it had the three-headed quarterback monster of Bill Kilmer, Bob Waters, and John Brodie, and coach Red Hickey rotated them every play. Hickey had the three stand at least five yards behind center to get a better survey of the land. A better survey meant a better chance to see where the defenders weren't. It worked out well for the 49ers. The three quarterbacks ran for more than 830 yards and 15 touchdowns in 1961.

When the three got hurt the next year, the shotgun went the way of the drop kick for 13 years. Landry remembered what Graham had done to his Giants teams when he had more time to decide where he wanted to make a play. In 1975, Landry had Roger Staubach at the helm, who was Otto Graham minus the Chuck Taylors. Staubach stacked up rushing yards, but he did it when he was forced to run. Landry put Staubach deep in the pocket to begin with to give the heady quarterback a head start on pass rushers and the defense that was being thrown at him.

That same year, the Cowboys cemented the shotgun's place in the NFL. Trailing by four with less than 30 seconds left, Staubach took the snap in the gun at the 50-yard line. He chucked the ball in the general direction of Drew Pearson, who was wrestling with Minnesota Vikings corner Nate Wright. Pearson won the rebounding contest and strolled into the end zone with 24 seconds left to give the Cowboys an improbable 17–14 victory and an eventual trip to the Super Bowl.

That play was made possible by the shotgun and by Landry. Like he did on the defensive front, Landry spotted trends before they became trendy. He drafted Ralph Neely and Rayfield Wright, both close to 270 pounds, and Dave Manders, who played center at 250 pounds, which was massive for those days. "His vision for the game was superior," former Giants assistant Allie Sherman said at the time of Landry's firing in 1989. "Organizationally he was sound and conceptually he was more than sound."

THE GAME NO ONE WANTED TO PLAY

It was one of those "I remember where I was" days. The kind of moment our generation associates with the Challenger explosion and September 11. The kind the previous generation has long associated with Dallas.

On November 22, 1963, President John F. Kennedy was making the rounds in Dallas-Ft. Worth when he turned the corner at Dealey Plaza. Shots rang out from the Texas Schoolbook Depository and, moments later, the president was dead.

Cleveland Browns owner Art Modell, who was on the practice field listening to a transistor radio, immediately went back to his office to watch the Kennedy news coverage and to make a phone call.

Modell called then-NFL commissioner Pete Rozelle and made a demand: "Trust me: Don't play those damned games."

Kennedy's assassination happened on a Friday, and the Cowboys were set to play in Cleveland two days later. In one moment, a garden-variety NFL game had the potential to turn into a garden-variety riot.

Overnight, Dallas had become the target of a nation's scorn. Rozelle, in a move he later called one of his biggest mistakes, decided the seven scheduled games would still be played despite a nation in mourning. When Modell heard the news, he turned from NFL owner to military commander. He stationed sharpshooters around the stadium and had armed guards on the roof of Municipal Stadium as teams took the field.

Cowboys players were refused services at hotels and restaurants, some saying they felt tainted. Bob Lilly called it the only game he never wanted to play. Don Meredith said, 20 years later, he felt like he was "going to the lions with the Christians."

Landry, a military veteran and dedicated servant to his country, said years later that he didn't even remember the score, a 27–17 loss. "There was such an emptiness in everyone's heart," Landry told the *Dallas Morning News* in 1982. "It was a game that wasn't played with much intent."

LANDRY LEGACY LINE

The formula is a simple one, and it applies across the sports landscape. Head coaches find and develop assistants they like to work with because that comfort and chemistry leads to stability at the top that, in turn and in theory, is passed on the players. If the head coach is able to develop that chemistry, those teams that didn't develop it come looking in your backyard for people who can develop it. Folks often came looking in Landry's backyard.

Mike Ditka, Raymond Berry, Dan Reeves, John Mackovic, Gene Stallings, Neill Armstrong, and Dick Nolan all coached for Landry before getting their own NFL gigs. Part of the reason was Landry stayed almost 30 years on the sideline. Landry also gave his assistants an enormous amount of responsibility

> **"Everything I did as a head coach I learned from Coach Landry."**
>
> [MIKE DITKA]

and, as Reeves said, the Cowboys had a lot of success. "There is no substitute for knowledge," Stallings said. "Coach Landry knew so much about football, but his advantage was that he knew how to teach it to players and coaches. As coaches, we picked up on that and eventually used it to our own advantages."

Landry's assistants had varying success stories in the league. Berry and Ditka opposed one another in the 1986 Super Bowl, with Ditka's Chicago Bears beating Berry's New England Patriots.

Berry only coached eight years, but he averaged eight wins a year with the Patriots. Ditka won 121 games in 14 years, and Reeves coached three teams before leaving the Atlanta Falcons in 2003. Nolan, Stallings, Mackovic, and Armstrong didn't have the same kind of success, even though Mackovic and Stallings found the college game more to their liking, with Stallings winning a national championship at Alabama in 1992.

Landry had his hands in all aspects of the Cowboys game plan, but he challenged his assistants to be the innovator he was. As a result, a lot of bright football minds developed under him. His attention to detail and consistency allowed him to replace the parts, but not the system. "Coach Landry prepared us so well," said Reeves, who spent 10 years alongside Landry. "There are very few times I can remember us being surprised or not ready for something."

"Everything I did as a head coach I learned from Coach Landry," said Ditka, who also played for Landry.

IT ALL COMES TO AN END

Jerry Jones has won three Super Bowl titles with the Dallas Cowboys. He is wildly wealthy, has tremendous influence among NFL peers, and has put his family's stamp on the organization.

Jones could win 10 more Super Bowls and rewrite the league's articles of organization. It wouldn't matter. He will always be known in Dallas, Texas, as the man who fired Tom Landry.

To be fair to Jones, he was coming in as a first-time owner looking to make his own splash. And, had the person he was replacing not been Tom Landry, Jones wouldn't have been treated like a pro football Grinch. In Dallas, teams are built to win Super Bowls. Landry hadn't been since 1978—10 seasons. His early 1980s teams were some of the best in the league, but the Cowboys lost three straight NFC title games between 1980 and 1983. The team missed the playoffs in 1984 but bounced back to the playoffs in 1985. In 1986, Dallas went 7–9, ending the team's amazing stretch of 20 straight winning seasons. That's when the talk started. Had the game passed Landry by? Had the man that had been such an innovator finally been caught up to? Two years later, the Cowboys had their worst season since 1960, the team's first in the league, going 3–13.

About that time, another set of hard times were about to send things in motion. Whispers were abound that Bum Bright, who had bought the team from the Murchison family five years earlier, had a desire to sell the team because one of his banks was failing, and he was ready to rid himself of the rigors of NFL ownership. So willing was Bright to get rid of the team that when an offer of a reported $10 million more that Jones was offering came in, Bright turned it down. He said he already had an agreement with the Arkansas oilman, though it was nothing more than a one-sheet outline of a deal. Bright said he wouldn't go back on his word. When he wouldn't, he sealed the fate of the Cowboys' only coach, something Bright has long said he regretted.

Deal in hand, Jones came to Dallas with an unexpected visitor in tow and headed to Mia's, a famous Mexican restaurant in Dallas. The *Dallas Morning News* sent a photographer to the restaurant after receiving a tip the two were there. The paper snapped a picture of the two dining, a now-famous photo that appeared in the paper the morning of February 25, 1989. Later that day, Jones stepped up to a Valley Ranch podium and formally announced he had bought the team.

Because he was still general manager of the team, Tex Schramm had to stand up in front of a shocked media gathering and announce something he probably never thought he would.

With tears flowing and a cracking voice, Schramm announced that Landry had been fired earlier in the day in a meeting at his Austin home with Schramm and Jones. Schramm added that Jones's dinner guest, University of

> **"It's very, very sad. It's tough when you break a relationship you've had for 29 years. That's an awful long time."**
>
> [TEX SCHRAMM]

Miami coach Jimmy Johnson, was taking over. "It was a very difficult meeting," Schramm said at the news conference. "It's very, very sad. It's tough when you break a relationship you've had for 29 years. That's an awful long time."

Landry didn't comment on the day of his firing. Two days later, he showed up in Dallas to give an emotional goodbye to his players. Like that day in Pittsburgh that turned the whole thing around, there were a lot of tears.

Although Schramm and Gil Brandt stayed with the new regime initially, neither had much of a future in Dallas. "I saw the writing on the wall," Brandt said. "Coach Landry was hurt by what happened, but I don't think he was ever really bitter about it." Landry may not have been bitter, but he let Jones know for almost five years just how hurt he was. In Cowboys lore, being inducted into the Ring of Honor at Texas Stadium is considered by some an even bigger honor than the Pro Football Hall of Fame. Landry went into the Hall of Fame in 1990 (some say Landry was the only consensus choice ever, though the balloting is private). The previous year, the year he was dismissed, he turned down

AP/WWP

ABOVE: Landry reacts to a missed pass to a wide-open Jackie Smith in the end zone during Super Bowl XIII.

Jones's request to enter the Ring. He continued to turn down anything Cowboys until, finally, on November 7, 1993, at the urging of Bob Lilly, Roger Staubach, Bob Hayes, and Lee Roy Jordan, Landry finally relented and returned to Texas Stadium to see a Cowboys game for the first time since he had been fired. "I felt it was time to do it," Landry said afterward, "and I think it turned out all right. [The Ring of Honor] is so much more of a personal thing [than the Hall of Fame]. I got a feeling in my stomach that I don't normally have."

Landry died from leukemia just over six years later. The Ring of Honor ceremony was the olive branch between the new regime and the Landry years.

Landry never publicly said anything negative about the situation or about Jones. But, Jones admitted on the 15th anniversary of the incident that he maybe should have handled things a little differently. "I had had a little media experience [when I was at Arkansas]," Jones told DallasNews.com, "but I completely underestimated what it was going to be like in Dallas.

"I had the opportunity to do it differently. Bum Bright said he would make all the changes I wanted before I bought the club. But I was advised that the heads-up way to do it was to address any changes face to face. I know that my gut was telling me that I needed to have a personal dialogue with Coach Landry... [The public relations companies I had retained] said they'd advised dictators and leaders of huge companies, but they'd never known what it was like to change 'America's Team.'"

"I think Jerry underestimated the power of the Cowboys," Brandt said. "And the love one city and one organization had for one man."

THE MAN

Danny White couldn't believe what he was being told. Landry handed the game-plan reins over to White and had asked if the injured quarterback could run things for a while. A dumbfounded White took the placard and watched Landry skip to the locker room.

A few minutes later Landry was back on the sidelines and back in control. It was a Monday night game in 1987 against the Los Angeles Rams, and the whole nation was watching. Apparently, not all were Cowboys fans.

When Landry returned, he gathered White for a quick conference. Landry let White know that stadium security had received a threat on Landry's life and that a sniper supposedly was in the crowd. Landry told White that for the rest of the game it would be better if he didn't stand too close to his coach.

White couldn't believe what he was hearing. A threat on Landry's life and the coach was still roaming the sidelines? "They wanted me to stay in the locker room," Landry told White, "but I persuaded them to let me wear a bulletproof vest and come back out."

> **"They wanted me to stay in the locker room, but I persuaded them to let me wear a bullet-proof vest and come back out."**
>
> [TOM LANDRY]

Calm and composed. That was Landry the man. A possible rifleman was sitting in the stands, and Landry still approached his craft with vigor. Even with a bulletproof vest on beneath his suit, Landry still had the unflappable stare and impenetrable personality. At times, the façade made him seem cold, someone without emotion. Landry said that wasn't it at all. That's just the way he learned to coach. "The way I trained myself to concentrate, I blanked everything else out," Landry told the *Dallas Morning News* in a 1989 interview. "I trained from watching Ben Hogan. He never let his concentration break."

The demeanor didn't always sit well with players. Landry had his run-ins with flamboyant types such as Thomas "Hollywood" Henderson and Duane Thomas, who had well-chronicled drug problems. Landry's regimented style wore some down, especially toward the later part of his career when the money and the athlete sense of entitlement grew substantially.

Landry once sat Hall of Famer Tony Dorsett because he hadn't let Landry know why he missed a light workout the morning of the game. It was Dorsett's rookie season. He was coming off a Heisman Trophy winning-season at the University of Pittsburgh, and his family, including mother and father, had flown in for a game. It didn't matter. Dorsett hadn't called, and he got benched—for a spell. Landry eventually put Dorsett in the game, but he embarrassed Dorsett in front of both his own and the Cowboys' family.

Landry, however, did have a soft and humorous side. During a training camp, Staubach wasn't faking long enough on a goal-line play to suit Landry so the coach told his quarterback to get out of the way and let a 40-something coach with a bad knee show him how to do it. Landry gimped to the right after faking and then told Staubach to run the play. He did, complete with the limping to the right after the fake. It was widely reported that there was a Landry smile on the practice field.

During his coaching career, Landry became a deeply faithful man. However, he never preached his faith to his players. That was one arena Landry didn't tread in. After his firing in 1989, Landry took a more active role in the Fellowship of Christian Athletes organization as well as the motivational speaker circuit.

In 1995, after he lost his daughter to liver cancer, he established the Lisa Landry Childress Foundation at Baylor Medical Center in Dallas to fund awareness programs for organ donors and transplant programs.

But, it was for the FCA where Landry, who has the stretch of Interstate 30 between Dallas and Fort Worth named for him, did most of his work after his career. He worked as many as 40 states in one year and spoke as much as he could in Dallas. "Tom Landry," the Reverend Billy Graham has said, "is one of the finest Christian men I know."

> **"I just looked forward to getting the team together every year and seeing how good we could make them by September."**
>
> [TOM LANDRY]

Legendary football coach, dedicated husband and father, respected among peers and those in the cloth. "I just did my job," Landry told the *Dallas Morning News* when asked about his lasting impact on the NFL. "I really didn't think about that. I just looked forward to getting the team together every year and seeing how good we could make them by September." That's the life of an icon. That was Tom Landry.

TEX
SCHRAMM

Tex Schramm wanted to make sure Lamar Hunt understood clearly. It was the Texas Ranger statue. The one in the lobby. At Dallas Love Field. "Meet me there," Schramm told his rival.

The Kansas City Chiefs and former AFL Dallas Texans owner told Schramm he would need to check his schedule, but he thought he had enough time to get together with the Dallas Cowboys' general manager for a quick chat. Hunt was on his way from Kansas City, where he was forced to move the Texans in 1963 after Schramm's Cowboys ran him out of Dallas, down to Houston to meet with other owners of the NFL's chief rival. He had a layover at Love Field, and Schramm was anxious to get negotiations started.

Schramm was at the statue as planned that April 4, 1966, morning. He said little to Hunt when they met. Schramm waited until the two got in his car in a dark Love Field parking garage.

Then, Schramm told Hunt they needed to talk business. Baseball was busy being the national pastime and putting football, both the AFL and NFL, on the back pages. Competition between the two leagues was about to get out of hand, and Schramm and his buddy, NFL commissioner Pete Rozelle, were concerned. The AFL was building stadiums and creating huge gaps between the haves and have-nots of their league by signing players, such as the New York Jets' Joe Namath, to ridiculous contracts. The NFL was churning as the premier football league, but some of its teams, the Redskins and Steelers in particular, were having a hard time paying their people.

These kinds of problems, Schramm told Hunt, were only going to get worse for both sides if the

TEX SCHRAMM

Born: June 2, 1920, in San Gabriel, California
Died: July 15, 2003
Position: President and General Manager
Years with the Cowboys: 1960–1989
Career Highlights:
* Developer of the NFL's first scouting system
* Co-coordinator of NFL-AFL merger in 1970
* Promoter of the six-division, wild-card style playoff system after the merger
* Chairman of the NFL Competition Committee, 1966–1988
* Proponent of miking officials wirelessly and using instant replay

Honors:
* Inducted into the Pro Football Hall of Fame in 1991
* Inducted into the Ring of Honor in 2003

two leagues didn't start talking seriously about merging. Hunt told Schramm he thought the AFL would be open to those talks.

Hunt then got out of the car, and on the plane to Houston, the wheels were now in motion for the massive NFL domination of the American sports landscape in place today.

Less than a month later, the two were back together, out of the dark and into the comfort of Schramm's Dallas home. Negotiations were going smoothly until the New York Giants pulled the rug out from the talks with the Buffalo Bills' signing of Pete Gogolak. Other AFL owners warned Hunt to not be lured by the smooth-talking Schramm. After all, Hunt had already lost the Dallas turf battle to Schramm. AFL owners didn't want him to lose the battle of the leagues.

Schramm found Hunt at the Indianapolis 500 and told him that he was alarmed by the signing but assured Hunt that those kinds of things were not indicative of how the NFL operated as a whole or how they would operate while negotiating the merger. Hunt took Schramm for his word.

Just over two months after placing the initial phone call and meeting in an airport parking garage, the AFL-NFL merger was complete. During the merger talks, Hunt came up with the idea that until the league became one big, happy family in 1970, the two factions should play a championship game between the two leagues. NFL folks were on board with the idea. Hence, in January 1967, the first Super Bowl.

One of the major parts of the merger, which Schramm insisted on, was revenue sharing among the league's teams. Pittsburgh and Washington were having trouble keeping financial pace as were several AFL teams. Although a merger may eventually have happened anyway, it may have happened after several teams went out of business. By insisting on a common draft and equal revenue sharing, teams competed on equal ground whether they were in Buffalo, Dallas, New York, or Kansas City.

Schramm, who had a journalism degree, also helped put the league in a prominent television position. When the full merger happened in 1970, *Monday Night Football* was created, deepening all owners' pockets.

To this day, the revenue sharing model keeps the Green Bays, New Orleanses, and other teams in smaller cities on the same footing as their larger city bunkmates. It makes for a competitive balance that baseball has yet to figure out.

That kind of forward thinking is why a chance phone call to arrange a meeting in front of a statue in a Dallas airport has created America's new pastime. "The National Football League continues to prosper from Tex's insight and innovation," Cowboys owner Jerry Jones said. "His fingerprints are all over today's game—from the sidelines to the yard markers, from the press box to the television trucks."

"Tex was such a builder," Hunt said. "He had this pride for the product. That made Tex special." It also made the NFL and football pretty special to a nation.

TAILOR-MADE TEXAN

It only seemed like the name was made up. How appropriate that the man running the Dallas Cowboys was a larger-than-life man with the name of a larger-than-life state. Although he was born in California, Texas E. Schramm was destined for Texas.

He was named after his father, a first-generation German immigrant, who took the "Texas" name because "as the 12th kid the family just ran out of names," Schramm used to quote his dad saying. Schramm's parents met in Texas but raised their son in California. Tex didn't get back to the Lone Star State until his college years. Even then, he didn't get to stay long.

He attended the University of Texas in 1941 before the air force and World War II came calling. He was back at UT four years later, earning a journalism degree and working at the *Austin American-Statesman*, a job that not only made Tex think he could write the column better than the sportswriters could, but also gave him an appreciation and understanding of how important the media was.

It was so important to Schramm that after graduating from UT in 1947, he moved back to California to take the Los Angeles Rams lead publicist job for $5,000 a year. In those days, baseball, in any form, dominated sports pages. Schramm got to know writers and editors and pleaded for any kind of space, even on the back page, for what his Rams were doing.

When not begging for ink, Schramm dabbled in scouting and Rams administration. He maneuvered his way around the organization, picking up odd jobs with the team when he could. Less than two years in to the PR gig, Schramm was named president of the team.

With Schramm's promotion, he had an opening for a media guy. The opening went to, in his first football job, future NFL commissioner Pete Rozelle.

Schramm ran the Rams from 1952 to 1957 before taking off for CBS. While still sowing his journalism oats at CBS, Schramm heard about a group trying to put together an expansion team in Dallas, headed by former MIT running back turned Dallas wealthy man Clint Murchison. Murchison had tried to buy the San Francisco 49ers in 1954 and bring them to Big D but was turned down. He made runs at the Chicago Cardinals and Washington Redskins but was told no dice. Finally, he put together a group to solicit an expansion club. That's when Schramm became interested.

In 1959, Schramm arranged a meeting and told Murchison he wouldn't mind a shot at turning an expansion team into a big-league franchise. Ten days later, the Tex Schramm era began.

PUTTING IT TOGETHER

Despite being a new owner, Clint Murchison learned that at least one aspect of real business translated to the sports business: You hire good people and stay out of their way. Murchison hired Schramm and told him to pass that philosophy down the Cowboys food chain.

Schramm, a fiercely loyal man, decided to go with what he knew. Having been the Rams general manager in the mid-1950s, he saw how the New York Giants were making a run to the top of the league with a dominating defense. He had heard stories about a hot-shot defensive coordinator named Tom Landry creating new schemes, new systems, and new ways of beating the Cleveland Browns. Schramm gave Landry a call. Both had South Texas roots, and both were Texas Longhorns. Both served in the military during World War II and were even in Austin at the same time. Schramm told the 35-year-old

Landry that he needed someone to come to Dallas and take complete control of the football side of things. Tex would take care of the showmanship and the business side of things, but a spot was available for a wall-to-wall football man. Landry accepted before the city even had a team. "There is one thing you must have in football: one continuous line of authority," Schramm once told the *Dallas Morning News*. "Tom knew he had authority over the players and everything that had to do with the playing of the game."

"We never had a close relationship, but that doesn't mean you can't be successful," Landry added. "Tex and I were in tune. . . . We just meshed well in the system we were using."

Schramm's next task was stocking the team. Like always, Schramm wanted to do something innovative in areas few others were thinking about. He had a guy in Milwaukee who had done some Big Ten scouting for him when Schramm was with the Rams. The guy created detailed scouting reports on players and, to Schramm, seemed to be on the cutting edge of involving technology in his scouting. The only issue was that Gil Brandt, the Cowboys' vice president of personnel development for almost 30 years, only dabbled in scouting as a hobby. He was a Wisconsin grad, liked living in Beer Country, and was earning nice cash snapping baby pictures.

BELOW: Tex Schramm was a forward-thinking innovator who transformed the Cowboys into "America's Team."

AP/WWP

ABOVE: Tom Landry and Schramm break ground for the new Cowboys practice facility in 1983.

Schramm, with his autonomy model in mind, told Brandt he would run the scouting department from end to end. No meddling from Landry. No meddling from him. Brandt asked where to sign and came south. The Cowboys' first holy Trinity was in place.

GET RID OF HIM PLEASE

Just because Schramm thought he could always beat the other guy didn't mean that it happened overnight. The first few Cowboys teams, well, they weren't good. Fans and media let Schramm know things needed to change.

After the 1964 season, coach Tom Landry had a 13–38–3 record. Schramm and owner Clint Murchison called a news conference to announce something regarding their coaching situation. Reporters gathered in the room and started being reporters. There was no speculation among this group. Figuring out who was replacing Landry was already the hot topic.

Following his mandate to stay out of the way, Murchison asked Schramm his thoughts on Landry's performance. Schramm told him he wouldn't have hired Landry in the first place if he didn't think he would eventually turn the franchise into a winning one.

Murchison agreed. He stepped to the podium that day and announced the team had just signed Landry to a 10-year contract extension. "I'm sure there were a lot of surprised reporters in that room," Landry told the *Dallas Morning News* after he was fired in 1989. "It came as a surprise."

THOSE HAYES AND STAUBACH GUYS LOOK GOOD

One of Brandt's trademarks was finding free agents everyone else overlooked. Schramm's contribution to the department was taking speedsters in the late rounds of the draft, just to see what would happen.

In 1964, with Landry firmly in place, Schramm thought he'd give a couple of guys a shot in the later rounds of that year's draft. In the seventh round, he thought he'd add a little speed to the roster, grabbing Robert Hayes, a Florida A&M sprinter who had put up a 9.1 in the 100-yard dash. Hayes wasn't eligible to sign with the league and had no plans to do so. He was training for that year's Olympics in Tokyo.

Hayes won the gold medal in the 100 meters at the 1964 Olympics. He also signed with the Cowboys, showing up in 1965 as Bob Hayes, the man who, because of his speed, forced the creation of the zone defense.

Three rounds later, Schramm took that year's Heisman Trophy winner, Roger Staubach of Navy. Staubach fell so far because he had another year at the Naval Academy and then a lengthy military commitment after school. Schramm didn't care. He was worth a gamble at that point. "Staubach?" Schramm asked in the *Dallas Morning News* the day after the 1964 draft. "You'd have to say we're building for the future. He ought to be a fine rookie in 1994."

Staubach showed up a little earlier. He put on a Cowboys uniform in 1969 and turned into a Hall of Famer.

WELL IT WORKED ONCE

Schramm took a shot on another sprinting Olympian in 1984 when he took multitime gold medalist Carl Lewis in the 12th round of the 1984 draft. Lewis never signed, but a gamble a year later ended up paying dividends for both Schramm and the new regime.

In the 1985 draft, Dallas spent a fifth rounder on running back Herschel Walker, who had already signed with the United States Football League's New Jersey Generals. Walker ended up with the Cowboys a season later after the USFL folded. Walker had 1,574 total yards and 14 touchdowns in 1986. In 1988, he ran for 1,515 yards, the fifth-most ever by a Cowboys runner.

Jerry Jones bought the team after that season, and new coach Jimmy Johnson thought it time for Walker to go, despite him being the Cowboys' only true, proven veteran. The Cowboys traded him to the Minnesota Vikings for a bevy of draft picks, one of which turned out to be Dallas' next great runner, Emmitt Smith.

SOPHISTICATED SCOUTING

Former president Ronald Reagan used to say in regard to any information he received about the former Soviet Union that the United States should, "Trust but verify, but don't be afraid to see what you see."

Cowboys scouting man Gil Brandt was never afraid to see what he saw. But, he had some nice technological advances to help verify his trustworthy eyes.

While working for CBS and pushing for the first televised Winter Olympics (Squaw Valley in 1960), Schramm was introduced to the computer. He was so taken by the amount of information that could be produced and how quickly it could be done that he was certain his scouting department could use the machine to their advantage.

Schramm got with IBM and developed a program that wasn't helpful insomuch as it told the team who projected well to the NFL, but, rather, who didn't.

In 1977, Southern California running back Ricky Bell was wowing everyone except the Dallas computer. The computer said don't worry that Bell would be taken No. 1 overall by the Buccaneers. The better player would be available to them.

That better player was Pittsburgh runner Tony Dorsett.

YOU WILL LISTEN TO ME

Former Cowboys defensive back Cornell Green used to say that Schramm treated contract negotiations like Schramm was having to give out his own money. And that was if you could get in to see the Cowboys general manager.

One year, Staubach thought it was time for a new contract. He just didn't realize how hard it was going to be to make Schramm part with cash. Not long after the 1964 draft, Staubach had sat with Schramm in a hotel room and scribbled out a future contract on a legal pad that said Staubach would participate in training camp when he had built up enough naval leave.

The setting for this contract negotiation would be quite different. Staubach made his way to Schramm's office and knocked on the door. Schramm grumbled something about being on the phone and told his All-Pro signalcaller to hold his horses.

Schramm was on the phone with his old buddy NFL commissioner Pete Rozelle. As Schramm's conversations with Rozelle always were, this one wasn't short. Staubach sat in the lobby growing ever impatient.

Finally, Staubach had enough. He walked outside the office and slid out a window to the ledge outside Schramm's office. With Schramm looking out the window and toward a busy expressway, Staubach, a few stories above ground and only inches from the edge, jumped in front of Schramm's window.

Tex gulped, but the conversation didn't end. "I just saw my future quarterback flash before my eyes," Schramm told Rozelle. Moments later, Staubach got his meeting—inside the office.

WELL, YOU'RE NUMBER ONE, TOO

Schramm was famous for being the only NFL general manager listed in the phone book. After the final roster was set, the team, at Schramm's directive, gave the media a complete home address and phone number directory of players and coaches.

But just because Schramm used to be a sportswriter and understood the importance of the media didn't mean it was always smiles and giggles covering Schramm.

Retired *Dallas Morning News* writer Bob St. John, who penned Schramm's biography, wrote in a column after Schramm's death in 2003 that he showed up one Saturday before a Cowboys game in Philadelphia, at Schramm's urging, to

> **"I just saw my future quarterback flash before my eyes."**
>
> [TEX SCHRAMM]

work on the book. Schramm was showing his legendary temper that day. He was mad because the scotch wasn't right. He was mad the Penn State game in Pennsylvania was on instead of his Texas Longhorns. (This was before DirecTV.) St. John knocked on the door, and Schramm looked at him and yelled "What the [expletive] do you want?"

St. John lost his cool, yelled back, and flipped Schramm the finger.

In typical Tex fashion, though, everything was eventually cool. "We both laughed about it the next morning," St. John wrote.

AP/WWP

ABOVE: Schramm greets coach Tom Landry (right) in 1959. It was the beginning of a lasting legacy.

For all Schramm did with the Cowboys, the large majority of his fan base will always be grateful for his 1972 creation of the Dallas Cowboys Cheerleaders.

Going to college at Texas and having covered his share of high school games while writing in Austin, Schramm knew how influential actual cheerleaders could be for creating fan excitement.

What Schramm understood better than most is that the NFL product was entertainment. People went to and watched the games as an escape from their normal lives. Schramm made sure that escape became a full-blown show.

A big part of Schramm's show and a continued big player in current Cowboys land is America's Sweethearts, the Dallas Cowboys Cheerleaders. When Schramm created the cheerleaders, he didn't have megaphones and poodle skirts in mind. He had hot pants and hotter women with the hottest athletic bodies on the brain. He had already gone just the good-looking woman route. In the 1960s, Schramm had models work the sideline. They looked great, but they didn't do anything else.

He had also gone the other way. Up until 1971, the CowBelles & Beaux were a group of high school students that cheered on the locals.

During the spring of 1972, Schramm brought Texie Waterman on board to teach a group of lookers how to become part of the spectacle. Waterman was a Dallas-area choreographer and, like everyone else Tex brought on board, worked in tune with Schramm. Waterman choreographed pregame routines that made the girls a major part of the show. Of the 60 who showed up for the original tryout, seven were picked.

Eventually, the cheerleaders became their own attraction. In the 1970s, the group was part of two made-for-TV movies. Today,

> **"The reality is that Tex sacrificed the Cowboys' good for that of the league many times."**
>
> [GIL BRANDT]

their swimsuit calendar sells well and the shooting of the calendar makes nice programming for ESPN.

IMPACT STILL FELT

The next time you buy a Terrence Newman jersey or a Bill Parcells "Tuna" t-shirt, think of Schramm. As he was walking through the locker room one day, Schramm noticed stacks of mail in each player's locker. Wanting to get the mail cleaned up so the locker room looked better, Schramm had a few staff go through the players' mail. The team would respond to the letters, often including a black-and-white 8x10 photo. Over time, Cowboys fans talked to other Cowboys fans that had received the pictures. A groundswell of desire for the pictures began, and suddenly Schramm knew he had another money-maker. He took the idea to the league, suggesting that each team communicate with fans like this and that it be coordinated through the NFL. That branch of the league today is NFL Properties, itself worth millions. "A lot of people thought we got treated better because of what Tex did for the league," Brandt said. "The reality is that Tex sacrificed the Cowboys' good for that of the league many times."

Schramm is the one who suggested putting the goalposts in the back of the end zone. It took away from the greatness of the awkward player-goalpost collisions on NFL Films, but it provided more offense and discouraged the powerdown that is the field goal. Sudden-death overtime? A Schramm creation. Wireless mikes on the refs so the crowd knew what penalty had been committed? Schramm. The stricter pass defense rules so receivers had more liberty to operate? Instant replay's infancy? Yep, Schramm.

Within the organization, Schramm created the Ring of Honor at Texas Stadium to honor Cowboys greats. Some of those honored say the Ring means more than the Pro Football Hall of Fame. Ironically, Schramm never saw his own induction, dying on July 16, 2003, almost three months before being honored.

Schramm even had an impact on NFL tradition. In 1966, Rozelle was looking for a national game on Thanksgiving Day to follow the Detroit Lions' traditional turkey dayer. Schramm said that when he was at Texas, the Longhorns always played the heated rivalry game with Texas A&M on Thanksgiving and it was a huge event. So, he figured, why not take that scene to the professional level? Schramm told his old buddy the Cowboys were in. They were the only team that offered to take the game.

> **"As commissioner, I have benefited greatly from what Tex had a big hand in creating."**
>
> [PAUL TAGLIABUE]

For all the great contributions that Schramm made to the actual game, his biggest innovation is still impacting the business of today's NFL. Schramm had seen Houston build the Astrodome, shielding fans from the elements. When Texas Stadium was designed, Murchison wanted his team to play outdoors. The two compromised with the famous hole in the Texas Stadium roof. The sun still shined brightly, and fans were partly shielded from the elements.

In between the upper and lower decks of the stadium, Schramm talked Murchison into including an upscale area for fans to watch the game with groups. Schramm then started marketing his new suites to businesses in the area as places to bring special clients. With the idea, the luxury box era began. "As commissioner," NFL commissioner Paul Tagliabue said on the day of Schramm's death, "I have benefited greatly from what Tex had a big hand in creating."

"He was a competitor and loved to argue," said Gene Upshaw, executive director of the NFL Players Association. "But he had a lot of class and you always knew he was trying to do what was best for the NFL. We were on opposite sides of the negotiation table and he was always firm in his beliefs, but Tex and I had respect for each other. He played a big part in getting us to where we are today."

LEAVING THE COWBOYS

The Cowboys just don't seem the same without Schramm. Even now. The Jones family has owned the team over 15 years, and many faces and many philosophies have passed through Valley Ranch since Schramm left in 1989. The team's image will always be Landry, but the Cowboys are the Cowboys, "America's Team," because of Schramm.

Schramm wasn't let go on the night Jones bought the team. But he knew it was coming, especially because he found out about the sale while watching television. Schramm was with Jones that day in Austin when Landry was fired. It was Schramm who stood teary-eyed that night in front of the Dallas media as the regime change was announced.

Not two months later, Schramm had had enough and resigned. He took over as president of the World League of American Football, a league that was eventually absorbed by the NFL to become the NFL Europe development league. As one friend put it, Schramm thought of the world first and then the United States. It was this thinking that had Tex being Tex in his WLAF position. That didn't sit well with some of the board of directors members, and Schramm was gone from the league in less than a year and a half.

Schramm still attended Cowboys games, but he didn't have much to do with the new era. When Schramm was elected to the Pro Football Hall of Fame in 1991, his acceptance speech revealed the humility of a man who had just spent 40 years competing in a fiercely fought arena. But, he admitted that day, he was proud of what he had accomplished and that it was important to him how history would judge him. "I would like to have gone out with the '80s being like the '70s," Schramm told the *Dallas Morning News* that day. "Nonetheless, I'm proud of the 20-year run of winning seasons, the five Super Bowls. . . . I don't have any bitterness as far as the new [Cowboys] are concerned. They have their opportunity for their own era." Because from 1959 to 1989, that era of Cowboys and NFL football belonged to Tex Schramm.

DON
MEREDITH

Tom Landry got up on New Year's Eve 1967 feeling somewhat chilly. The team was in Green Bay preparing for the NFL Championship against Vince Lombardi's Packers. Landry knew it was going to be cold. The team arrived the night before in 20-degree weather and clear skies above. The Cowboys were prepared for chill. They weren't prepared for frozen.

Landry had heard all about the Packers' new $80,000 electrical heating system they had put under the field to warm the earth. The sun could have been under Lambeau Field, and playing conditions still would have been cold.

The team was staying in a hotel whose doors opened to the outside. Landry got up that morning, dressed, and prepared to go out for breakfast. He opened the door expecting about 20 degrees. He got close to 20 degrees— below zero.

"I couldn't believe it," Landry told the *Dallas Morning News* in 1989. "It was like the North Pole. You can imagine the shock. I think we were in shock most of the game."

Cowboys quarterback Don Meredith may have been the biggest hit. Meredith was a born-and-bred Texan. Even though he was a chiseled NFL veteran and had played his share of cold games, Meredith had never played on an ice sheet. There weren't a lot of hockey rinks in Meredith's hometown of Mount Vernon, Texas.

The vaunted electrical heating system hit the skids before the game kicked off. Mix in a cold front that swooped down from Canada around 3 a.m. and a nasty wind that put chills close to –50, and you've got yourself the famous Ice Bowl. The game that spawned Lambeau Field's "Frozen Tundra" nickname.

For Meredith, it was a game, and a season, better forgotten.

The year before, the Cowboys had lost in the title game to Green Bay. That one hurt, but Landry later admitted Lombardi's troops were the superior team. He didn't feel that way in 1967. This was supposed to be Dallas' year. Landry felt the Cowboys were the better team. He just had miserable conditions.

Meredith threw for only 59 yards on 10–25 passing, slinging the ball, as *Dallas Morning News* writer Bob St. John wrote in the next day's paper, like he was "throwing a wet brick with a long stick." Meredith didn't even throw the Cowboys' best pass that day.

That came on the first play of the fourth quarter when Dan Reeves, on a play called "fire pitch," threw a halfback pass to Lance Rentzel to put Dallas up 14–10. Meredith had a pass intercepted and a costly fumble.

Early in the second half, Meredith led the Cowboys from their own 11-yard line to the Green Bay 22. On a designed play, he scrambled nine yards to the 13-yard line, where the ball slipped out of his hands and into those of Herb Adderley, the same guy who picked him off earlier in the game.

The Ice Bowl will always be remembered for Packers quarterback Bart Starr's one-yard plunge with 13 seconds left to give Green Bay its third straight NFL title. For Meredith, the legendary game was a reflection of his Dallas career: brilliant at times, but, in the end, the media's favorite fall guy. "It's most disappointing to have this happen twice in a row," Meredith said after the game. "I guess we can do everything except win the big one."

YOU WILL BE A COWBOY

Meredith didn't have a choice. He was going to be a Dallas Cowboy. Meredith was a star at Mount Vernon, about two and half hours east of Dallas. Growing up, he saw legends Doak Walker and Kyle Rote running over people for SMU at the Cotton Bowl. Walker and Rote combined to form one of the greatest 1–2 punches in college football history in the late 1940s. As the duo was putting SMU on the national college football map, Meredith was becoming an East Texas legend.

He took his legend to Walker's and Rote's stomping grounds, arriving just after Raymond Berry and Forest Gregg took off. Meredith's first season was the first for new SMU coach Bill Meek. Meek knew he had a talent in this kid from the East Texas Piney Woods, but he didn't know how much Meredith could do. In Meredith's first year, he set a Southwest Conference record by completing 70 percent of his passes. He also pulled a Doak Walker, returning kicks and mixing in punting and placekicking.

DON MEREDITH

Born: April 10, 1938, in Mount Vernon, Texas

Died: December 5, 2010

Nickname: "Dandy Don"

Position: Quarterback

Years with the Cowboys: 1960–1968

All-Pro/Pro Bowl Appearances: 0/2

Honors:

* Named NFL Player of the Year in 1966
* Cowboys record: Three 300-yard passing games in a season (tied)
* Cowboys record: Five touchdown passes in one game (tied, set three separate times)
* Cowboys record: Longest pass completion (95-yard pass to Bob Hayes on November 11, 1966)
* Inducted into the Ring of Honor in 1976

Seeing the versatility he had in Meredith, Meek installed a four-wide receiver look in 1958, using two on the outside and two in the slot, a skeleton version of today's run and shoot. Meek put in the offense so Meredith would have more room to improvise.

In the first season of the new offense, Meredith was an All-American, the first of two selections. "I don't think I've ever seen a fellow dominate a game like Meredith does," former Georgia Tech coach Bobby Dodd said of Meredith's college career. "Self-confidence just stands out all over him. When he walks onto the field, it's like he just says, 'Never fear, Meredith will get it done.'"

During the 1959 season, Dallas banking magnate Clint Murchison began putting a group together to get an expansion team to Big D. Whenever Dallas got its team, Murchison knew who he wanted leading it. He wanted Mount Vernon's favorite son. The NFL wanted that as well.

At the time, the league was fighting a fierce turf war with the AFL. The NFL didn't want Meredith anywhere near the rival league. So, instead of Meredith going into the 1960 draft, the league assigned Meredith's rights to Murchison's group. All the group had to do was get him inked. Just in case Meredith didn't sign, the Chicago Bears spent a third round pick on the SMU quarterback.

DON'S DANDY HOUR

Murchison got his team and his man, signing Meredith to a "personal services" contract, believed to be worth over $100,000 for three years. "I had the best contract in football," Meredith said the day he retired. "[Cowboys general manager] Tex Schramm reminded me of that every time we talked about it."

Cowboys coach Tom Landry said the most difficult decision of his Dallas career was choosing Meredith over Craig Morton and Jerry Rhome in 1965. Meredith had been with the team since its inception in 1960, but Landry didn't feel a quarterback, even the most seasoned of college ones, was ready for the league until he had at least three years of sideline experience.

He didn't have that much time with this young team, giving Meredith significant time in 1962 and handing the reins over to Meredith the next season. Then, the team continued to look for a Meredith replacement. The Cowboys picked up Roger Staubach and Jerry Rhome in the 1964 draft and spent a first rounder on California quarterback Craig Morton in 1965. Despite getting torched in the media and hearing whispers from fans after Meredith's combined 26 touchdowns-24 interceptions performance over the 1963 and 1964 seasons, Landry stuck with Meredith in 1965. "I know that there are many who disagree," Landry said at the news conference the day Meredith retired, "but I still feel firmly that the decision in 1965 to go with Don was the most important one made by this team and led directly to the conference championships in 1966 and 1967."

In 1966, "Dandy" Don rewarded Landry by leading the Cowboys to their first ever playoff birth. Meredith avoided injury for one of the rare times in his career and lit up the league. He completed 51 percent of his passes, threw for more than 2,800 yards and 24 touchdowns, and ran for five more.

He led Dallas to four straight wins to open the year. The Cowboys ended it by wining five of six, with Meredith sitting out the season finale because the Eastern Conference title was already in hand.

The next week, "Dandy" was back on the field, this time bringing championship football to the Cotton Bowl for the first time. The Cowboys started the game in awe of the mighty Packers and the situation. The NFL title was on the line, and Dallas walked into their own stadium looking like wide-eyed fans. The Cowboys fell behind 14–0 in the first quarter and trailed 34–20 with 5:20 left.

> "I had the best contract in football. Tex Schramm reminded me of that every time we talked about it."
>
> [DON MEREDITH]

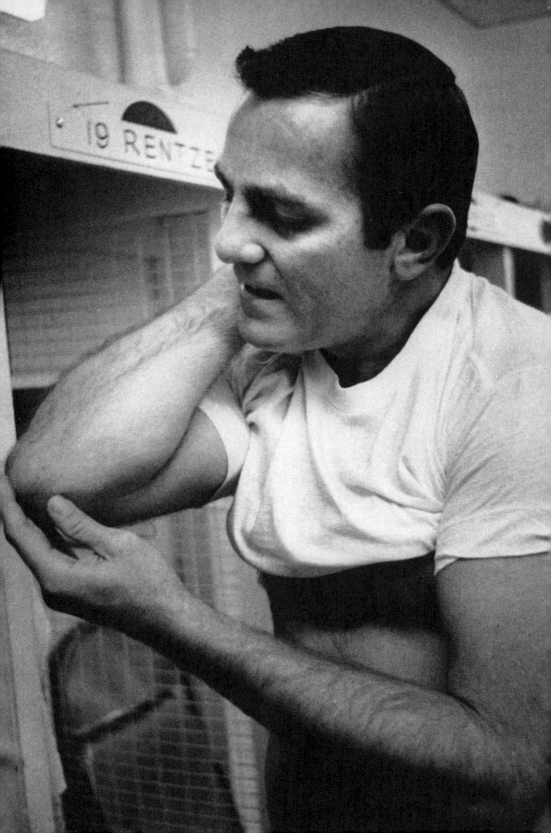

Then, Meredith realized he was the 1966 NFL Player of the Year. He hit Frank Clarke for a 68-yard touchdown, and Dallas was in business. The Cowboys got the ball back with 2:19 left at the Green Bay 47-yard line. Three plays later, Meredith went to Clarke again, this time in the end zone. Not wanting to give up a touchdown, Packers defensive back Tom Brown brought Clarke down. Pass interference, sure. NFL title-saving play, absolutely.

On fourth down, with 45 seconds left, Meredith scrambled to his right and once again looked for Clarke. This time, Brown didn't have to interfere. He picked the ball off and snatched yet another title for the Packers.

The game was a heartbreaker for Meredith and the Cowboys and a bittersweet ending to a turning-point year. It was the final play of the Cowboys' and Meredith's best season. Meredith was the top player in the league, and the season started a run of six straight division titles.

INFIRMARY MEREDITH

That Meredith even played in the Ice Bowl was a testament to the Mount Vernon tough man. During the 1967 season, Meredith got pneumonia, broke his nose and ribs, and twisted his knee. And it all started before the real games began.

Meredith broke a rib on his right side against Baltimore in the final preseason game. The next week, Dallas was opening in Cleveland's Municipal Stadium, the Cowboys' own little shop of horrors. Before the game, there were questions surrounding Meredith's availability. Apparently no one asked Meredith about it.

Meredith started and led Dallas to a 21–14 win, Dallas' first ever against the Browns. He threw for 205 yards and two touchdowns and stayed in the game even after Jim Houston clobbered Meredith's blind side, slamming into the right side of his body. Meredith played three more games with the fractured ribs, including throwing a last-second touchdown pass to Dan Reeves to beat the Redskins.

The next week Meredith finally went to the hospital to get the ribs checked out. Doctors confirmed the breaks, also telling Meredith the reason he had felt

LEFT: Although Don Meredith's career was plagued by injuries, he was known for his physical and mental toughness.

so weak recently was because he had pneumonia. Meredith spent the next three weeks on the sidelines watching Craig Morton and Jerry Rhome lead the offense.

Meredith returned to lead the Cowboys to a 37–7 win over Atlanta, but his ailments weren't over. Earlier in the year, while checking out his broken ribs, Meredith quipped to a group of reporters that he was thankful that he had never had nose issues. Check that, "Dandy." Against Philadelphia, Mike Morgan crushed Meredith, sending him to the very familiar Baylor hospital.

Six days later, complete with a plastic mask, Meredith was under center in San Francisco for one series. On the Cowboys' second set, Meredith twisted a knee and had to come out.

Showing the guts that made him a Cowboys legend and the stubbornness that made him a whipping boy, Meredith trotted on to the Cotton Bowl turf just over a week later on Christmas Eve night against the Cleveland Browns. He completed 10–12 passes for 212 yards and two touchdowns to put the Cowboys into the title game against Green Bay.

DONNING THE YELLOW JACKET

Meredith did and continues to do things on his terms. He was only 31 when he retired in 1969, leaving the game because he said he didn't want to "feel like a man going to play golf without all his clubs."

Instead, Meredith hit the bricks for Hollywood and, eventually, a legendary role alongside Howard Cosell on *Monday Night Football*.

For all Meredith accomplished as a quarterback, the nation will always remember "Dandy" Don as the witty, down home, everyday guy answer to the elitist, high-minded commentary of Cosell on *Monday Night Football*. Cosell would be using big words to describe the simplest of two-yard out patterns, and Meredith would call him on the carpet for not simply calling it like it was: now second and eight.

The chemistry was beautiful. It made Meredith a household name, Cosell a legend, and *Monday Night Football* the most successful television program in history.

The Cowboys' loss was the NFL's and ABC's gain. Meredith retired in 1969, the program was created in 1970, and the run was on. Meredith was a booth fixture for the first four seasons before leaving for a four-year run on NBC's pro coverage. Meredith returned to ABC in 1977 and stayed until 1984. However, it was those first four years that catapulted the Meredith and Cosell duo into the American consciousness.

Cosell was famous for his temper, Meredith for his laid-back quick hits. Even when Cosell allegedly showed up inebriated for a contest and threw up on Meredith's boots, Mount Vernon's favorite took it in stride. He also provided some of the greatest lines for *Monday Night* viewers in the program's history.

Meredith was the original William Hung, endearing himself to a nation by declaring games over with a very hard to listen to version of "Turn Out the Lights, The Party's Over."

During a game in which in the Houston Oilers were getting blown out, cameras panned the disinterested stadium looking for something interesting. Cameras found a fan sleeping and immediately focused on him. When the fan realized he was on television, he flipped the bird for all of America to see.

"Well," Meredith said to Cosell, Frank Gifford, and a watching nation, "that guy thinks his team is number one!"

Speculation has been that producer Don Ohlmeyer fed Meredith the dandy line. Doesn't matter. No one could have delivered it like Meredith.

Early in the show's career, the crew was doing a Cleveland game. The Browns had a wide receiver named Fair Hooker, who played six years, averaging more than 20 catches a season. On this night, Hooker caught a pass and then caught Meredith's eye.

"Fair Hooker?" Meredith asked, pausing for a second. "Never met one."

THE ENIGMA

History has judged Meredith's time in Dallas as one of the city's greatest sports regrets. Meredith was a native son, born and bred Texan. He was a college football legend in the city where he worked. He was the one that led an expansion team to back-to-back NFL title games. Still, the city, and especially the media, never embraced Meredith the way it has its other sports legends. Maybe it was Meredith's down-home approach to the game and to life. There were other things important to Meredith. That attitude was in contrast to the football-only lifestyles of coach Tom Landry and general manager Tex Schramm. That contrast led to media types casting Meredith as an under-achiever. That casting was passed on to the fans. No Cowboys player who contributed so much has ever been so jeered by those who were supposed to be his own.

Meredith had his share of disappointments and a rash of injuries. He threw an interception on a desperation fourth-down throw on the last play of the 1966 NFL Championship Game. He had a key fumble in a forgettable performance in the Ice Bowl the next year. Still, the Cowboys were in their infancy, still finding their NFL legs. The team made back-to-back champion-ship game runs six years into their existence. And, yet, Meredith was never the focal point of those teams until something went wrong.

Meredith retired after the 1968 season, which was one of his best. He completed 55 percent of his passes, the best mark of his career, racked up 21 touchdowns, and had the best quarterback rating of his career. Still, he was the target of any and all Cowboys fan frustration. Meredith's performance often gave credence to the catcalls. His daring style led him to taking a lot of chances. For his career, he completed 51 percent of his throws, but for his 135 touchdowns there were 111 interceptions. He had costly plays in big games and was the quarterback when the Cowboys lost to Cleveland in the 1968 playoffs, more ammunition for those calling the Cowboys the NFL's bridesmaid.

Dallas lost only twice that regular season and was riding a five-game winning streak heading into Cleveland's Municipal Stadium. Meredith struggled in the first half, throwing an interception that led to a field goal, but still keeping the wheels on enough to scratch out a 10–10 halftime tie.

On the Cowboys' first two second-half series, though, the wheels came off in earnest. Dale Lindsay picked off the first one, taking it back 27 yards for a score. On the next set, Meredith looked for Lance Rentzel. Rentzel couldn't handle the pass, knocking it straight to Ben Davis. One play later, Leroy Kelly took it 35 yards for a 24–10 lead.

Gary Cartwright later wrote that Meredith's last professional play may not have been his fault: "According to Landry's gospel, the Cleveland defensive back who intercepted Meredith's final pass should have been on the other side of the field. Unfortunately, the Cleveland defensive back was in the wrong place. It wasn't that Landry was wrong. Cleveland just wasn't right."

"This was a game you couldn't blame on Dandy Don. Meredith did a perfect job every time he held for a place kick."

[THE *DALLAS MORNING NEWS*]

Either way, Meredith was crushed, pulled for Craig Morton, disheartened, and headed for retirement.

Such a cruel ending for someone that suffered such cruel attacks in his career from the mouths of fans and the pens of writers. Although he never said anything publicly, the written scorn he received showed how mighty a sword the pen can be.

When asked his opinion on the greatest Cowboys quarterback, Bob Lilly said his choice is Roger Staubach. However, "Mr. Cowboy" added, "I would include Meredith right there, if he hadn't just gotten killed in those days."

Game stories in Dallas papers from those years crucified Meredith.

• "Don Meredith, whose pro career has been a toe-to-toe battle with the winner-loser syndrome, seems destined to play Hamlet," read a story in the *Dallas Morning News* after the 1968 loss to Cleveland. "Meredith, who had led Dallas to its most impressive victory ever—52–10 smashing of Cleveland last season for this same title—was indecisive and never quite with it here. Because he's the quarterback, he will naturally—and it fits—wear much of the burden of this defeat on his shoulders."

• "This was a game you couldn't blame on Dandy Don. Meredith did a perfect job every time he held for a place kick," from a 1965 story in the *Dallas Morning News* after a loss to Philadelphia.

• From the Ice Bowl game against the Packers in 1967: "Don Meredith, who just could not throw in this weather, was trapped just once behind fine protection and this was because he failed to read a key on linebacker Lee Roy Caffey. . . . Don hit only 10 of 25 for 59 yards and [Packers quarterback Bart] Starr, more used to the cold and a guy who could throw under any conditions, was better."

• From the *Dallas Morning News* after a 34–31 loss in 1966 to Washington: "Although Meredith missed half the game, it's doubtful he could have made much difference."

• Meredith couldn't escape the wrath even in wins or when the intent was complimentary. After a 38–24 win over the New York Giants in 1967, the *Dallas Morning News* wrote: "Meredith was high on his first two throws—you could hear the boos again—but then he brought his sights down to dead center . . . Oh well, Meredith now has a new baby boy, born Friday night after a delay which seemed almost as long as the Cowboy offense in this coming year, and a heckuva start in the NFL's first two games."

Meredith chalked up the criticism to playing a high-profile position and the fact he was really the only well-known football star on a new team. It took time to develop a dislike for other players. But, when the guy leading the team has been on the local football radar screen for almost 15 years, it's easy to blame the familiar.

"I guess no other player has been exposed, maybe overexposed, as I have [been] at the Cotton Bowl," Meredith lamented after a game during the 1968 season referring to the place he played both his Cowboys and SMU home games. "I guess they think I'm part of the stadium."

The treatment may not have led directly to Meredith's retirement, but several that played with him said they thought it played a major role. Meredith was always upbeat, never confrontational toward fans or media. Even on the day he retired, Meredith refused to say the climate had anything to do with it, although he did pause before answering.

"As far as the people of Dallas are concerned, well, an awfully lot of them have been very good to me," Meredith said. "In 13 years of football here, I have a lot

> **"The fond memories and the good friends, those are the things I want to remember."**
>
> [DON MEREDITH]

of good friends, and I think a lot of fans, too. The fond memories and the good friends, those are the things I want to remember."

The treatment didn't cause Meredith to become an immediate recluse. He had a long television stint with ABC and NBC and commercials with the Lipton tea company before finally settling to a quiet, private life in the Santa Fe, New Mexico, area until his passing on December 5, 2010, at age 72 after suffering a brain hemorrhage.

The back porch wisdom spewing, "Hey, that guy would make a really cool uncle" Don Meredith the nation got to know on *Monday Night Football* was simply never embraced during his playing days.

"The Cotton Bowl may have been The House Doak Built," Meredith used to say, referring to the SMU star who played before Meredith in the Fair Park stadium, "but I paid for it." It will long be the city's greatest sports regret.

BELOW: Meredith guided the Cowboys through some of their most legendary games, including the Ice Bowl against the Packers. Still Meredith was constantly a target for blame from fans and the media.

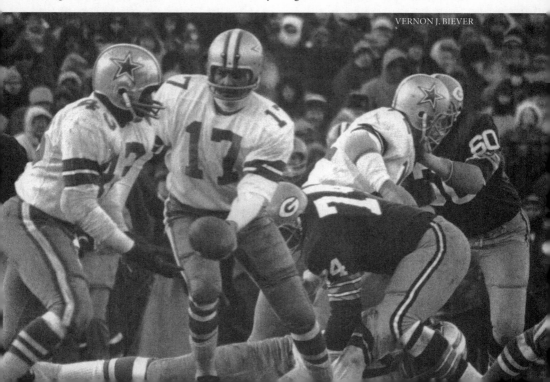

VERNON J. BIEVER

BOB
LILLY

Bob Lilly lived a Texas dream that no one else ever will. He grew up in small-town Texas idolizing Southwest Conference legends. His play at Texas Christian University eventually made him one of those legends. He was the first draft choice ever of what would become "America's Team," the first member of the Cowboys' Ring of Honor, one of the greatest defensive linemen of all time, and both a college and pro football Hall of Famer.

That's Bob Lilly, "Mr. Cowboy."

Lilly was born in Olney and raised in Throckmorton, about three hours west of Dallas. Like any Texas kid in the late 1940s and early 1950s, Lilly was raised on high school football and the Southwest Conference. Friday nights were spent following the locals wherever around the state. Saturdays were spent in the fields, listening to the Southwest Conference *Game of the Week* on the radio in between tending to the crops and the wells. In those days, Southern Methodist University's Doak Walker and University of Texas' Bobby Layne were carving out national names and making dreamers out of every kid that ever put on shoulder pads in a dusty Texas town.

Understand this about small-town Texas, especially small-town West Texas: people are real, and the work is tough. It still is today and was, especially, in Lilly's day. Folks put in full days and expect their neighbors to do the same. The common struggles create camaraderie and lasting memories and instill a pride and work ethic that only someone from those parts understands and appreciates.

Lilly's parents moved from Throckmorton to Pendleton, Oregon, before Lilly's senior year in high school. It was a one-year respite. Lilly was back in Texas the next year, putting on the TCU purple in Ft. Worth and starting his run as one of the all-time great Texas football legends. "He would, in fact, serve as the poster boy for his generation of aspiring young athletes," one writer wrote during Lilly's TCU tenure. "He was a product of the time when virtually every talented schoolboy with Texas roots dreamed of playing in the Southwest Conference."

FRIGHTENING FROG

There was no greater time in college football than when the Southwest Conference existed. National college football was one animal, and then there was the sideshow that was the intrastate Texas rivalries. There never before was and, because of the current college structure, there never will be another set of fierce rivals in such close proximity. It was a day when the small, private schools (TCU, SMU, Rice, and Baylor) were on equal football footing as the big daddies, UT and Texas A&M. It was a day when coaches from those private schools could walk into a schoolboy's bedroom, sweet talk momma, and put the fear of God into an Aggie or a Longhorn recruiter. When it came to Saturday afternoon, those same schoolboys who said yes to the SMUs and TCUs of the league put that same fear into fans and players of their larger counterparts.

Lilly and his future Cowboys teammate Don Meredith were large reasons TCU and SMU became and remained college football big wigs in those days. And although they fought a common battle against the larger Texas schools, some of the SWC's grandest battles were fought between those two Texas legends.

In 1959, Meredith was on his way to his second consecutive All-America season while TCU was on it way to the Cotton Bowl as SWC champs. Against SMU that year, Lilly lived in the Ponies' backfield. He made 11 tackles, blocked a punt, and recovered two fumbles. Lilly and his Frogs harassed Meredith and the Mustangs' vaunted spread offense to the tune of minus one yard of offense. It was Meredith's worst collegiate game and Lilly's finest hour.

The next year, Meredith was assigned to the first-year Cowboys while Lilly was racking up a consensus All-America team senior season. A season later, the two rivals became Cowboys teammates.

Lilly was a novelty for that time in the college game. At 6-foot-5 and 250 pounds, he was a rough, hard-nosed player who could run. He had no problem sneaking around the outside from his defensive tackle spot and running

BOB LILLY

Born: July 26, 1939, in Olney, Texas
Nickname: "Mr. Cowboy"
Position: Defensive Tackle
Years with the Cowboys: 1961–1974
All-Pro/Pro Bowl Appearances: 7/11
Honors:

* Cowboys record: 11 Pro Bowl appearances
* Named to the NFL 75th Anniversary Team
* Named to the AFL-NFL 25-Year Anniversary Team
* Inducted into National Football Foundation Hall of Fame
* November 23, 1975, declared "Bob Lilly Day" in Dallas, Texas
* Inducted into College Football Hall of Fame
* Inducted into the Ring of Honor in 1975
* Inducted into the Pro Football Hall of Fame in 1980

down the fleetest of running backs. And there hasn't been an offensive lineman born yet who could stop an in-his-prime Lilly. He had the rare combination of being fast and, in today's terms, lean. But anyone who ever saw Lilly play said there was no one stronger than the ole boy from Throckmorton. "Let me tell you something about Bob Lilly," a former teammate said during Lilly's TCU days. "If I was as big and strong as him, I would charge folks just to live."

THE FIRST COWBOY

Someone was going to have to wear the distinction. Tex Schramm and Gil Brandt just wanted to make sure it was someone who could handle the label of being the first player the new Dallas Cowboys franchise ever drafted.

Upon the retirement of the team's first pick in 1975, coach Tom Landry called Lilly "the greatest player I've ever coached." Sounds like Schramm and Brandt made a nice pick, even if it wasn't technically the Cowboys' first ever.

Back in the day when scouting was jumping in your truck, checking out a few local boys, and taking the word of folks in far-off locales, the Cowboys struck hometown gold. Lilly was an All-American at TCU in Ft. Worth and right in the Cowboys' backyard. The Cowboys just had to make sure he was still available for the picking.

The Cowboys had two first-round picks in 1961. The team's first ever choice, the second overall, had been traded, along with a sixth-round pick, to

Washington the previous year for quarterback Eddie LeBaron. That pick turned into Wake Forest quarterback Norm Snead.

So, in their first draft day ever, the Cowboys watched. They watched as Hall of Famers Mike Ditka (Bears), Jimmy Johnson (49ers), and Herb Adderley (Packers) were all swiped off the board before they came back up at No. 13.

> # "I was just happy to get out of that game alive. I'll never forget that game."
>
> [BOB LILLY]

At that point, there was no debate. The Cowboys wanted a defensive stalwart for their defensive-minded coach. Lilly wasn't the only defensive or Southwest Conference player Dallas drafted that year. The Cowboys drafted 20 rounds, picking five SWC players among their first seven choices. Of the 17 players taken, five made the active roster, only one of which didn't go to a SWC school.

Lilly, Baylor's Sonny Davis, UT's Don Talbert, SMU's Glenn Gregory, and Long Beach State's Lynn Hoyem all made the team from that first draft crop. The only SWC alum that didn't become a Cowboy was the team's second ever draft choice, legendary Texas Tech linebacker E.J. Holub. Holub shunned the NFL, signed with the rival Dallas Texans of the AFL, and became a Kansas City Chiefs great.

STILL REMEMBERS

Lilly knew it was a gamble, but he knew it was coming. The Cowboys had been here the previous year and saw their championship hopes dashed in the end zone at the Cotton Bowl when Don Meredith was intercepted on fourth down on the last play of the Cowboys' season. It was now a year later, and a Dallas-Green Bay face-off for the NFL title had again come down to the last play. This time, the scene was Lambeau Field, the Packers less than a yard from a second straight title and the most miserable weather conditions ever for a football game, a stark contrast from the previous year's Cotton Bowl game.

Green Bay was trailing 17–14, and coach Vince Lombardi had no time-outs after he stopped the clock with 16 seconds to discuss with quarterback Bart Starr how the Packers were going to get the ball in the end zone. With the weather like it was, Starr didn't want to throw the ball. He told Lombardi he could run the quarterback sneak, 31 Wedge, and get in. Against the Doomsday Defense and one of the all-time defensive fronts? Starr said the field was so frozen that if he could just get a step or two of traction, there was no way Dallas could move quickly enough to corral him.

As Starr walked out of his meeting of the minds with Lombardi, Lilly got ready. With breath smoking through his facemask Lilly started marking his territory. He took his cleats and scratched them against the frozen turf. Like a batter digging into the box, Lilly entrenched himself in his self-made holes. At the snap, Lilly fired off but seemed a step slow. Later, in his book *Instant Replay*, Packers guard Jerry Kramer wrote that the play was to stay as far away from Lilly as possible. He and Kenny Bowman were supposed to move Jethro Pugh. Kramer wrote that he came off the ball faster than he ever had, admitting that he couldn't say for certain that he wasn't offsides while leading Starr into the end zone.

No flag, no title for the Cowboys, but a situation Lilly still remembers. "I see that clip fairly often, me digging in trying to get a little traction for the sneak that I was certain was coming," Lilly said. "I was just happy to get out of that game alive. I'll never forget that game."

MR. INTENSITY

Lilly could have made money doing something else. Probably a lot more money doing something else. As a first-round pick, Lilly made $11,000 as a rookie in 1960. For that, the Cowboys got the NFL's Rookie of the Year and the foundation of their Doomsday Defense.

The key ingredient to their foundation's fire was a legendary intensity that showed whether Lilly was playing cards or slapping around offensive linemen. Lilly simply didn't like to lose, something the Cowboys did a lot of early on.

It was Lilly who stepped up in 1965 after a game against Pittsburgh in which the Cowboys played poorly and in which Landry thought was the beginning of his own demise. With a weeping Landry standing in the locker room and telling the team how he thought his multiple offense look and the Flex defense was still going to revolutionize the league, Landry said he wasn't sure he would be around to watch it happen. Lilly rallied the team around their coach, dug down, and finished with a flurry, making the playoffs and keeping their coach's job. "We reached down and got it those last 12 games," Lilly said. "We gave something a little extra. Had we not, I'm not sure he would have come back."

Ever since his Throckmorton days, Lilly was defined by his intensity. It was so well known around the league that the NFL created a "Bob Lilly: Intensity" poster in 1971. The shot is of Lilly with teeth clenched and face focused on ripping Buffalo Bills running back Wayne Patrick's head off.

Lilly attacked his craft with the same intensity. Lilly was immensely strong naturally. The arrival of Landry's specialized strength and conditioning coaches made Lilly unstoppable. Teams tried double and triple teams, zone blocking, and specialized schemes. It didn't matter. Lilly neutralized them; one because of his strength and two because he spent hours in the film room studying offenses and blocking techniques, combining a ruthless field intensity with a voracious appetite for learning.

Intensity also kept Lilly on the field. He missed one game in a 14-year career that saw him make a franchise-record 11 Pro Bowls (10 straight between 1964 and 1974) and seven All-Pro teams. It also inspired a memorable moment that defined Lilly's competitive nature.

"The competition is what I love. That makes me a little more intense. Personalities don't enter into it at all. My objective is to get the man with the ball, [and] nobody better get in my way."

[BOB LILLY]

For years, the Cowboys were branded the original Buffalo Bills, the ones that could get to the edge of the promised land but never were able to take the exit off the highway. In 1970, the Cowboys finally got to Super Bowl V, playing against the Baltimore Colts. Doomsday was doing its thing. Chuck Howley, the game's MVP, picked off two passes, Mel Renfro got one, and the Cowboys picked up three Colts turnovers. However, the offense couldn't keep pace. Penalties at inopportune moments, receivers running the wrong routes, and an interception by linebacker Mike Curtis, which gave Baltimore a first down at the Dallas 27-yard line with 1:09 to play, put Dallas again at the edge of heartbreak.

With five seconds left, Jim O'Brien, a rookie kicker wearing No. 80, sent the Cowboys and Lilly over the edge. As the ball went through, Lilly saw yet another chance for a title slip by. He took a couple of steps, ripped his helmet off, and threw it further than any Cowboys' pass that day. "The competition is what I love," Lilly once said during his career when asked to describe what made him a cut above other linemen. "That makes me a little more intense. Personalities don't enter into it at all. My objective is to get the man with the ball, [and] nobody better get in my way."

FINALLY GETTING ONE

Chuck Howley was running around pulling a Jim Valvano, looking for someone to hug and telling anyone who would listen that the oldest Cowboys' player was just getting started. Lilly stood in the locker room and lit up a big, fat victory cigar.

Two longtime Cowboys had finally won their first league championship. After losing to Green Bay in 1966 and in the Ice Bowl of 1967 and in Super Bowl V the previous year, the Cowboys finally got the title so many had been predicting.

It was a 24–3 demolition of Miami at New Orleans' Tulane Stadium in Super Bowl VI, still the only Super Bowl in which one team failed to get to the end zone. It was a day dominated by the Doomsday Defense and a Lilly play that still stands out in Super Bowl lore. The Cowboys' front seven of Lilly and

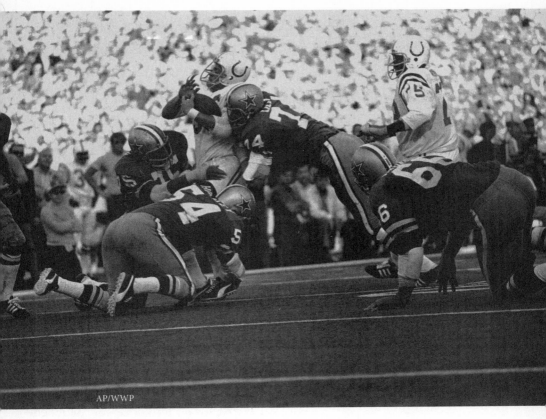

ABOVE: Lilly (74) and company corral the Colts in Super Bowl V, forcing three turnovers. However, offensive mistakes led to a heartbreaking last-second loss.

Jethro Pugh at tackle, George Andrie and Larry Cole at end, Dave Edward and Howley at outside linebacker, and Lee Roy Jordan in the middle had terrorized teams all season. Against a Miami offense that featured Bob Greise, Larry Csonka, Jim Kiick, and Paul Warfield, the Dolphins were held to 185 total yards. Griese threw for 134 yards and technically rushed for zero yards. But, that was back in a day when sacks didn't count against your rushing yards. Had they, the Dolphins total offense and Griese's rushing yards would have looked even worse.

On the play, Griese dropped back looking for someone to break free deep in the Dallas secondary. The Dolphins needed something big to happen, and Griese was convinced he could get someone downfield if he just kept the play

> **"In my lifetime, there hasn't been a player as good as Bob Lilly. And I don't expect to ever see another one. He is the greatest player I've ever coached. He's that once-in-a-lifetime player."**
>
> [TOM LANDRY]

alive. He didn't count on Lilly being able to keep up. Griese snaked, scrambled, and scattered. He twisted and turned, looking for anyone to take a pass. Lilly kept pace, never going for one of Griese's slick moves. Lilly finally put Griese on the ground for a 29-yard sack, still the biggest loss in Super Bowl history.

ON THE OTHER SIDE

When Bob Lilly made the Kodak All-America team in 1960 at TCU, little did he know the sponsor's gift would have a lifetime impact. He was given a 35 millimeter camera and 200 rolls of film and was told to start snapping.

That was the genesis of a hobby that has now become a passion. So much of a passion that Lilly got together with retired *Dallas Morning News* writer Sam Blair, who covered some of the early Lilly teams, to write *Bob Lilly Reflections* in 1983. Lilly used the film to take candid shots of teammates in situations where a normal photographer would not have access. There were shots on the team bus, of guys hanging out, and of players in humanizing situations.

Lilly's career spanned from the expansion years to the first Super Bowl to the legends of the legends, such as Roger Staubach and Don Meredith. He began taking the pictures his rookie year, basically trying to get rid of the film. He has since moved into the digital realm, using scanners, a high-resolution printer, digital cameras, and a litany of field cameras from different companies.

His photography love is landscapes. He's shot all over the country, from Oregon wheat fields to a Maine lighthouse, from a New England farm to a Mesa Verde sunrise.

LILLY'S LEGACY

Many consider Bob Lilly the greatest defensive player of all time. The *Sporting News* ranked him as the 10th best football player ever, the third-highest rated defensive player behind former New York Giants linebacker Lawrence Taylor and Chicago Bears linebacker Dick Butkus.

Lilly was a seven-time All-Pro, the Rookie of the Year. He went to 11 Pro Bowls in a 14-year career and was on the AFL-NFL 25-year anniversary team and the NFL's 75th anniversary team.

With the Cowboys, he holds a lot of firsts. The first Cowboys draft pick in 1961. The first Cowboys player elected to the Hall of Fame in 1980. And the first inductee into the Ring of Honor.

Lilly retired in 1975, and general manager Tex Schramm was looking for a way to honor Lilly and future Cowboys greats. He brought Lilly back to Texas Stadium, put him in full uniform, paraded him around the stadium, and put his name in the "Circle of Honor" just underneath the Texas Stadium press box.

Present were aspects representing all of Lilly's NFL life: Chuck Howley, representing old teammates; Lee Roy Jordan, Schramm, Landry, and owner Clint Murchison, representing the current group; and former Green Bay Packers lineman Jerry Kramer, who may or may not have been offsides in the Ice Bowl, representing Lilly's opponents.

Lilly's No. 74 is also the only number Cowboys equipment folks frown on giving out. Although no number is officially retired, no one else has ever worn No. 74, and it's widely known why no one better ask for it. "In my lifetime, there hasn't been a player as good as Bob Lilly," Landry said at the Ring of Honor ceremony. "And I don't expect to ever see another one. He is the greatest player I've ever coached. He's that once-in-a-lifetime player."

LEE ROY JORDAN

Even now, the box score just looks wrong. Surely something was out of line. Maybe a friendly stat keeper, the fact that Oklahoma was a run-at-all-costs team, or maybe a nice-looking girl was in the stands he was trying to impress? Whatever the reason, Lee Roy Jordan's 31-tackle performance against Oklahoma in the 1963 Orange Bowl jumps off even this legend's bio. Thirty-one tackles for one man? "If a runner stayed between the sidelines," Alabama coach Paul "Bear" Bryant said after Jordan's performance in the Crimson Tide's 17–0 win over the Sooners, "he stopped him."

"He's never had a bad day. He was 100 percent every day in practice and 100 percent in the games."

[PAUL BRYANT]

The performance came with Joe Namath leading the Alabama attack, Sooners coach Bud Wilkinson coaching what would be his final bowl game, and President John F. Kennedy watching his last college game in person. Ten months later, he would be assassinated in Jordan's new hometown.

Alabama came into the game with a 9–1 record and having allowed 39 points in 10 games. No team had scored on the Tide more than once in a game. Had Alabama not lost to Georgia Tech 7–6 earlier in the year, Bryant likely would have been playing for his second straight national title. Instead, the fifth-ranked team in the land brought their smashmouth defense to Miami to play the eighth-ranked Big Eight champions.

The marquee matchup was Oklahoma's Joe Don Looney, one of the nation's leading rushers, against Jordan and a unit that was riding a stretch of 24 games of giving up seven points or less. The streak wasn't getting broken in Jordan's final Alabama game. The Sooners twice marched inside the Crimson Tide's 10-yard line in the first quarter, both times thwarted because of fumbles. After those drives, Oklahoma got little and Looney never got going, rushing for six yards on 10 carries.

While Jordan was rolling it up on defense, Namath was making his national spotlight debut. The sophomore, playing in his first season on the varsity, completed nine of 17 passes for 86 yards and a touchdown, the game's opening score.

But this was Jordan's night. The Tide handed Wilkinson his only Orange Bowl defeat in five trips, and Jordan ended his Alabama career with a record-setting performance that still gets talked about in Tuscaloosa. "He's never had a bad day," Bryant later said. "He was 100 percent every day in practice and 100 percent in the games."

'BAMA'S BAM!

Jordan's march to the Cowboys wasn't unlike Bob Lilly's. While Lilly grew up in rural Texas dreaming of playing in the Southwest Conference, Jordan did the same dreaming, just of a different conference and from a few hundred miles east.

Gene Stallings, a former Alabama head coach and Cowboys assistant, used to say that the difference between football in Alabama and football in other states is that people in Alabama simply don't care about any other sport. They care about their college football, and they care about it 365 days out of the year. "I can guarantee you that I can go to any town in Alabama right now, in the middle of the summer, whenever," Stallings said. "And someone will be talking Alabama football. Someone will be talking Auburn football. And, someone will certainly be talking Alabama versus Auburn."

This was where Jordan came from. He came from small-town Alabama dreaming of playing in an Iron Bowl game. Kids in those days in those parts didn't dream of the NFL. They dreamed of helping the locals take out their rivals. For Jordan, it was about taking a new Alabama coach and helping him turn legendary.

Paul "Bear" Bryant arrived in Tuscaloosa in 1958. The next year, he had Jordan on campus and the march was on. Bryant had already spouted off that he would win a national championship. In 1960, Jordan was on an Alabama team that tied Darrell Royal's University of Texas team 3–3 in the

LEE ROY JORDAN

Born: April 27, 1941, in Excel, Alabama
Position: Middle Linebacker
Years with the Cowboys: 1963–1976
All-Pro/Pro Bowl Appearances: 2/5
Honors:
* Cowboys record: 21 tackles in a game (1971)
* Cowboys: 2nd in career tackles (1,236)
* Cowboys: 2nd in solo career tackles (743)
* Selected to Cowboys Silver Season All-Time Team in 1984
* Inducted into the Ring of Honor in 1989

Bluebonnet Bowl. Jordan didn't just start as a sophomore; he led a Crimson Tide defense that stifled the Longhorns, much-hyped running game. He did so much stifling that he was named the game's most outstanding player.

As a junior, Jordan helped "Bear" keep his promise. Early in the year, Bryant had called his players "the sissiest bunch I've ever had." Jordan, who played linebacker and center, and his teammates took the criticism to heart, ratcheting things up early in the season and never letting up until Bryant had the first of his six national titles.

In the fifth game of the season, the Tide gave up three points in a 34–3 win over Tennessee. Alabama then put up five straight shutouts before Arkansas managed three in a 10–3 Tide win in the Sugar Bowl. During the six-game stretch to close the year, Alabama outscored opponents 161–3.

So much for sissies.

Jordan continues to be revered in Alabama. He is at the top of the list at a place that has produced names such as Namath, Hutson, Starr, Newsome, Hannah, and Stabler. Every spring, Alabama honors the Jordan legacy by handing out the Lee Roy Jordan Headhunter Award, given to the hardest hitting 'Bama player during spring practice.

When the end of the century rolled around, Jordan's name started popping up again in college football circles. He joined other former Cowboys Roger Staubach, Tony Dorsett, Bob Lilly, Randy White, Herschel Walker, and Deion Sanders as members of the Walter Camp All-Century Team. Recently, *College Football News* named him the 32nd best college player of all time. "He was one of the finest football players," Bryant said of Jordan, "the world has ever seen."

SHOW ME THE MONEY...
PLEASE

Cowboys general manager Tex Scrhamm didn't deal well with interme-diaries. If you went straight to Tex to do your business, you had fewer problems than someone who tried to send someone to take care of your business. But not all problems were solved because you had a one-on-one sit down with Schramm. The concerns were simply minimized. During the age before col-lective bargaining and players making Bolivia gross national product-like cash, Schramm's player contract dealings were one on one and to the point.

He developed a reputation as a hard ass, a well-deserved one for anyone that saw the some-times cantankerous Schramm at work.

Jordan had his run-ins with Schramm, especially late in his career. Feeling he wasn't getting his fair due in a contract negoti-ation, Jordan walked out on the team a few days before a season opener. Schramm was furious, holding a grudge that was never fully resolved.

> **"I do long for the good ole days. Something like [what we had] will never happen again."**
>
> [LEE ROY JORDAN]

Jordan felt those contract negotiations were one sided. There was no doubting the first contract the Alabama All-American signed with Dallas was, well, all Tex-sided.

Jordan was the sixth pick in the 1963 draft, a spot that now commands an eight-figure signing bonus. Jordan's bonus was only a seven-figure one, seven figures if you include the decimal point and the two zeros after the $5,000. He would make $17,500 as a rookie and get a $1,000 raise for each of the next three seasons. "Back then, we didn't have anybody to represent us," Jordan told the *Dallas Morning News* during a Ring of Honor roundtable before Schramm was inducted in October 2003. "When I signed my first contract for $17,500 a year, there weren't many ways to split that up. Coach 'Bear' Bryant was my agent at that time. He said, 'Boy, I'd sign that. That's a lot of money. That's a lot more than I'm paying my coaches.'"

Oh, but Jordan also got a car. Kind of.

Part of the deal was that scouting director Gil Brandt would bring Jordan the car in Tuscaloosa so Jordan could drive it and his things back to Dallas. Somewhere along the way, Brandt wrecked the vehicle, plowing into a cow. When he got to Alabama, though, he did not offer a new ride to his new middle linebacker. "So," Jordan told the *Dallas Morning News*, "I had a new wrecked car and $5,000."

Jordan said he should have negotiated like former running back Walt Garrison. "He got a horse trailer as his bonus," Jordan said, "and he still has it."

THREE AMIGOS

The Dallas Cowboys of the 1990s built their dynasty because they traded Herschel Walker in 1990 at the peak of his value to Minnesota for the Metrodome and all of the Vikings' draft picks until 2010.

Not true. Dallas actually didn't get the Metrodome. But the draft picks the Cowboys did get seemed to go on forever. Back in the day, Dallas didn't think as highly of draft choices. The Cowboys had the second pick in the 1961 draft but had it traded before they were even a team. In 1963, Dallas didn't trade its first selection. But, the team thought so much of the guy they did pick and the player they got by trading some later picks that the team just started throwing around draft choices like Monopoly money. It was the only time Schramm allowed anything to be thrown around like play dough.

In that draft, the Cowboys had the sixth pick, using it on Jordan. They packaged their second- and ninth-round picks to Chicago for the rights to

RIGHT: As a cornerstone of the Doomsday Defense, Lee Roy
Jordan took care of anything that came his way over the middle.

a bum-kneed linebacker that had called it quits during the 1959 season. Chuck Howley, a 1958 first-rounder, turned out to be a pretty nice find for Schramm and the boys, teaming with Jordan and Dave Edwards for 12 years to form the linebacking side of the Doomsday Defense. Although most of their success came in the "Next Year's Champions" era, when the Cowboys made it a habit of losing in next-plateau-reaching games, the trio finally broke through in Super Bowl VI, crushing Miami 24–3 and the "Will they ever do it?" whispers.

That was a different era of pro football. There was no salary cap, no parity, no vanilla games, no vanilla teams, and no vanilla players like today's NFL. The three played alongside one another because they enjoyed it and because each knew his own success was significantly based on the talents of the other two and the team in general. In today's game, one good season after a major injury, a player is looking to renew his deal, forgetting that nobody wanted him the year before when he was considered damaged goods.

> **"[The field at Texas Stadium] was in pretty good shape today other than for the cornerbacks and the guys who played wide. The edges of the field were still a little slippery."**
>
> [LEE ROY JORDAN]

Jordan said he knows the days of a unit sticking together like he, Edwards, and Howley did are long gone. That doesn't mean he wouldn't like to see them return. "I do long for the good ole days," Jordan said. "Something like [what we had] will never happen again."

Two seasons after the Cowboys drafted Jordan and traded for Howley, Howley was a Pro Bowl pick. A year later (1966), Jordan joined him, starting a four-year run where both were on the squad. Jordan also made the Pro Bowl in 1973 and 1974.

Playing together that long, the three developed a chemistry the game is likely to never see again. Edwards and Howley patrolled the outside, knowing that Jordan would take care of the middle. Jordan concentrated on the running game and rushing the passer because he didn't have running back containment concerns. Edwards and Howley would keep anyone from getting around the edge. Jordan got so involved in stopping the run that he set Cowboys tackling records that still stand. Jordan was also able to get involved with any receivers coming over the middle. Although pass coverage rules were much more liberal in those days, Jordan was a player in zone or man-to-man coverage. He twice led the team in interceptions because he only had to worry about what was coming over the middle.

Landry always called Jordan the catalyst of the Doomsday Defense. He was certainly the most steady. Only Bill Bates and Ed "Too Tall" Jones played more years in a Cowboys uniform than Jordan. No one started more consecutive games than Jordan's 154.

NEW DIGS

For the longest time, Cowboys fans have said that the hole in Texas Stadium provides the perfect opening for God to watch His favorite football team. Truth is the partial roof is the result of a compromise between Schramm and Clint Murchison. Both had been impressed with Houston's Astrodome, but Murchison thought football should be played outdoors. Tex thought an Astrodome facility might do well in a Dallas climate that can be brutally hot for September games. The compromise was a roof covered halfway. That way, Schramm's cheerleaders, patrons, and, most importantly, suite holders would be somewhat protected from the elements. The hole allowed the elements to become a part-time player.

Texas Stadium was a marvel in its day. And the Cowboys put on a marvelous performance when they opened it on October 24, 1971, by pasting the New England Patriots 44–21.

Jordan was a big reason Cowboys brass thought fans wouldn't mind the drive to suburban Irving to watch the team. On Texas Stadium's opening day, he sent the locals back to brutal traffic happy. He set up the team's first ever passing touchdown in the new building when he belted Patriots fullback Jim Nance at the New England 35-yard line. The ball rolled loose, and Jordan recovered it. On the next play, Staubach found Bob Hayes in the corner for a touchdown.

The Patriots were the perfect welcoming mat for the Cowboys' new digs. An inexperienced team with a rookie quarterback (Jim Plunkett from Stanford) playing one on its way to its first Super Bowl title. The new place was certainly impressive, but rain all week had made the surface somewhat slippery in spots, a problem that has continued to plague the stadium. The Texas Stadium field is built on a crown so that water drains away from the middle of the field and toward the seating area. From the sidelines, the view is like looking up a hill. From the middle of the field, it's like looking down a mountain. Eventually, those things became an advantage for the team. That first day, though, everything was new to everyone. "We were worried about the field all week," Jordan said afterward. "It was pretty slippery, which was probably because of all the rain we had this week. It was in pretty good shape today other than for the cornerbacks and the guys who played wide. The edges of the field were still a little slippery."

TOPPING THE CHARTS

Jordan was a tackling machine. Landry's Flex defense was predicated on Jordan getting to the football and shutting down the run. For 14 years, that was no problem for the Cowboys middle linebacker. Jordan retired in 1976, leaving with team records for total tackles, solo tackles, tackles in a game, and assisted tackles. Safety Darren Woodson has since passed Jordan's career, solo, and assisted tackles records, but even after almost 30 years what Jordan did in the middle of Landry's scheme is standing the test of time. Before Woodson, the closest anyone had come to Jordan's mark was end Randy White, who finished his 14 years with 132 less total stops than Jordan. White got closer to Jordan's solo tackle mark, falling 42 short of Jordan and now in third place after Woodson slid into first last season. Jordan still holds the team record for tackles in a game, falling short of his college record of 31, but still stopping 21 Philadelphia Eagles in a 42–7 win in 1971.

Jordan made the Doomsday Defense work because he was always around the ball. Some players have the physical gifts that allow them to over-power people and make a spectacular play here and there that draws attention. Playing just over 210 pounds, Jordan was small for a middle linebacker even in the 1960s. But, he was one of those "gnat" players that just seemed to be involved on every play. His 16 career fumble recoveries, tied for second most in team history, suggests he was often around the football.

Being a smaller linebacker, Jordan was able to keep pace with almost any running back or wideout that came through his area. He picked off 32 career passes and twice led the team in interceptions. His three picks against Cincinnati in 1973 are a team record.

"I'd like to thank Jerry Jones, the Dallas Cowboys, my friends, and the fans who remembered me for all these years."

[LEE ROY JORDAN]

Jordan was inducted into the Ring of Honor in 1989, the year Jerry Jones bought the team and cleaned house. Had Jones not ransacked Valley Ranch, Jordan would have waited much longer for his induction. In the summer of 1973, Jordan and Lilly skipped workouts because of contract problems with Schramm. Lilly got his issues worked out and lived happily ever after with the Cowboys' general manager. Jordan left the team, hanging the Cowboys out to dry with no middle linebacker. Schramm never forgot the bind, even though Jordan returned and made All-Pro that year. The problems lingered and created a strain that wasn't fully repaired until Jones came along and Schramm left the organization.

Not long after Jones bought the team, he needed something to bring folks to the stadium during the miserable 1–15 year in 1989. With Lilly's urging, Jones inducted Jordan into the Ring. When he made his acceptance speech

JOHN E. BIEVER

ABOVE: Jordan (55) set a high bar for future Cowboys defenders.

to the crowd, Jordan said he was happy he would now be alongside his buddies as Cowboys royalty, adding: "I'd like to thank Jerry Jones, the Dallas Cowboys, my friends, and the fans who remembered me for all these years."

Although Schramm was watching the festivities from a luxury suite, he wasn't thanked or invited to the field, making Schramm later admit a rare error. "I was going to put Lee Roy in the year I left," Schramm told the *Dallas Morning News* in 2000. "My one regret was not putting him in sooner only because I got angry."

Since his retirement, Jordan has joined Staubach and Howley as some of the more successful off-the-field Cowboys. In 1977, Jordan bought the Redwood Lumber Company of Dallas and renamed it Lee Roy Jordan Redwood Lumber Company. That Jordan has become a success in another arena probably wouldn't be a surprise to the man who brought him to Texas. "He was a great competitor," Landry said of Jordan. "He wasn't big for a middle linebacker, but because of his competitiveness he was able to play the game well. His leadership was there, and he demanded a lot out of the people around him as he did himself."

JOHN E. BIEVER

MEL RENFRO

Mel Renfro was going to make sure the score stayed baseball-like. He had to. For too long, he had seen things go the other way.

The Cowboys were leading the Detroit Lions 5–0 at the Cotton Bowl late in the fourth quarter of a first-round 1970 NFC playoff game. The difference was a safety, a 19-yard Mike Clark field goal, and Dallas not being able to turn 209 yards against the conference's best rushing defense into more points.

With every last-minute yard Detroit gained, the more the memories came back from the losses to Green Bay in the 1966 NFL Championship Game and the 1967 Ice Bowl, the more haunting the 1968 and 1969 Eastern Conference Championship Game losses to Cleveland became, and the louder the chant of "Next Year's Champions."

It was third and 10 from the Dallas 29-yard line. Lions quarterback Billy Munson dropped back and was looking dead in the direction of Earl McCullough. The pass was high, causing McCullough to jump. Had he stayed on the ground, the Lions would have had another shot at the end zone. Instead, McCullough did leave his feet, tipping the ball. Renfro was on top of the play. But instead of going for a bone crushing hit, he backed off and made a dive for the ball. With 35 seconds left and the cries of always the NFL bridesmaid and never the bride ready to rear their ugly heads, Renfro hauled it in, falling to the ground at the Dallas 17. The Cowboys had the win and, after beating San Francisco the next week in the final game at Kezar Stadium, a date with Baltimore in Super Bowl V. "As they were driving," said Renfro, who led the league in interceptions with 10 the year before. "I remember thinking about losing the previous four years in the playoffs, and here we were about to lose again."

Dallas had reason to think the NFL gods simply were not kind. On the final drive, the Lions yanked quarterback Greg Landry in favor of Munson, the only action Munson saw all day. On fourth and 10 from the Detroit 32-yard line, Munson went to McCullough for 39 yards down to the Dallas 29. The whole game, Greg Landry had thrown at Renfro. Each time, Renfro made a play. When Munson finally tried to go at him, Renfro made his biggest play. "I have been waiting for that one all season," Renfro said after the game. "I'm glad they threw at me."

The Cowboys were, too. The team had heard the catcalls from their fans and from teams around the league about being the guys that couldn't win the big one. Beating the Lions finally put Dallas on the path toward the Super Bowl. The win was especially sweet because the 1970 season really wasn't supposed to be a banner year. The team was break-

MEL RENFRO

Born: December 30, 1941, in Houston, Texas
Position: Defensive Back
Years with the Cowboys: 1964–1977
All-Pro/Pro Bowl Appearances: 5/10
Honors:
* Cowboys record: 52 career interceptions
* Cowboys record: 26.4-yard career kickoff return average
* Cowboys record: 626 career interception return yards
* Inducted into the Ring of Honor in 1981
* Inducted into the Pro Football Hall of Fame in 1996

ing in rookie running back Duane Thomas. Quarterback Craig Morton had off-season shoulder surgery and battled a badly cut hand the last two weeks of the regular season and the playoffs. There was internal strife over contracts, and a players' strike loomed. Lance Rentzel missed the last six games, Cliff Harris got an army call-up, and Calvin Hill was banged up all year. Even Cowboys coaches doubted this team was going very far.

In Week 9, St. Louis rolled into the Cotton Bowl for a *Monday Night Football* matchup. The Cardinals mauled the Cowboys 38–0, prompting the same Dallas fans that booed him into retirement to chant for Don Meredith, who was in the Cotton Bowl press box wearing the blazer of ABC's first-year *Monday Night Football* program. "I ain't getting back out there," "Dandy" Don said on the broadcast.

Meredith said that night that the Cowboys' biggest need was leadership. He questioned coach Tom Landry, Lee Roy Jordan, and Craig Morton. The questioning seemed fair for the now 5–4 Cowboys. The offense had six turnovers, special teams gave up a touchdown, and the Doomsday Defense had an off day. It was the last one they would have the rest of the year.

The next week, the Cowboys got off the deck with a 45–21 win at Washington. The win sparked a five-game winning streak to end the season, including a 6–2 win at nemesis Cleveland.

Dallas did give doubters more ammunition by losing Super Bowl V to the Colts on a tipped-pass touchdown and a last-second field goal by a rookie kicker. But, for that one day in the Cotton Bowl, the critics were put to rest. Even if some Cowboys players were slow to believe it. "[I didn't believe we had won] until I saw Mel on the ground with the interception," Jordan said after the game, "and I saw he still had the ball."

"That win," Renfro said, "lifted an enormous load off us. It put us over a big hump."

DESTINED FOR DALLAS

Dallas' darkest day destined Renfro for Big D.

No one has to be reminded what happened November 22, 1963, in Dealey Plaza. John F. Kennedy's assassination in Dallas sent a nation into mourning and forever marked a city. It also had quite an impact on a senior, two-way Oregon Ducks standout. Renfro was getting ready for the 1963 Civil War game against Oregon State when he heard the news. Renfro was dealing with the pressure of supporting a family while going to school and bearing the load of being the Ducks' biggest star. The news sent a fragile Renfro over the edge.

Renfro said he stepped out that night and hit the bottle. Several drinks later, Renfro picked a fight with a mirror that whipped him pretty good. The haymaker he gave the mirror left him with a severely cut wrist that came dangerously close to being more serious that it was.

The cut kept Renfro out of Oregon's annual Civil War game against Oregon State. He also missed the Ducks' 21–14 Sun Bowl win over Southern Methodist University, something Renfro's professional standing would later pay for.

In those times, scouting was part luck, part skill, and a lot of heresy. The Cowboys' Gil Brandt wanted to draft Renfro but knew the injury and Renfro missing two games would keep him out of the first round. "Probably could have gotten him in the third actually," Brandt said.

Before the 1964 draft, Renfro said Brandt and the Cowboys began spreading information about the injury, conjuring up stories to make it seem worse than it was. The Cowboys thought Renfro was such a damaged commodity that they spent their second-round pick on him.

Ah, the days of the genuine bait and switch.

NICE HAUL

There was absolutely no question who the Cowboys wanted in the first round of the 1964 draft. They wanted the University of Texas kid that had just won the Outland Trophy. Although they knew they would have to fight the AFL's Houston Oilers for tackle Scott Appleton, Brandt was determined that was a battle Dallas would win. Houston had drafted Appleton three days earlier in the AFL draft, but the Cowboys' decision was made. At No. 4, Dallas jumped, leaving future Hall of Famers Carl Eller and Paul Warfield, among others, on the board.

Appleton never played in Dallas, instead fleeing for the Oilers' cash. But things didn't turn out too badly for the blue and silver.

In the second round, the Cowboys grabbed Renfro. In the sixth round, they chose Georgia Tech's Billy Lothridge, a kicker and quarterback who, at the time, was the only Tech player to ever have more than 1,000 yards total offense. He set an NCAA record with 21 career field goals and finished second that year in the Heisman Trophy balloting.

> **"[I didn't believe we had won] until I saw Mel on the ground with the interception."**
>
> [LEE ROY JORDAN]

The Cowboys were so elated about getting Lothridge when they did; he was the first player they concentrated on signing, getting him under contract just hours after he had been selected. Focused on Lothridge, the team didn't have much to say about the seventh- and 10th-round picks that weren't even eligible to sign.

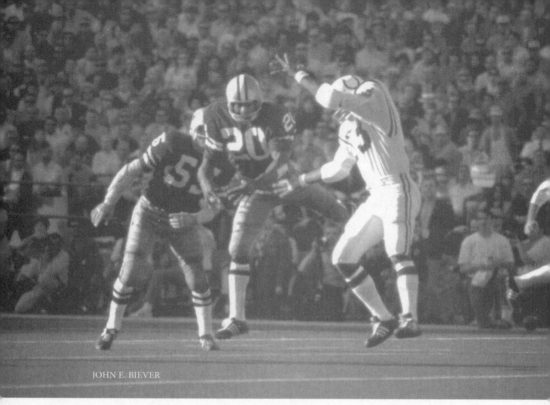

ABOVE: Mel Renfro (20) wreaks havoc on a Colts receiver in Super Bowl V. Renfro's disruptive presence made him a 10-time Pro Bowler and a Hall of Famer.

The seventh rounder turned out to be a Florida A&M sprinter named Robert Hayes. The 10th rounder: Heisman Trophy winner Roger Staubach of Navy.

Bob Hayes, Roger Staubach, and Mel Renfro: two in the Pro Football Hall of Fame, all in the Ring of Honor. All in one draft.

MOO MOVEMENT

Renfro had been a two-way star at Oregon. When he got to the NFL, Landry made sure any plans for Renfro on offense were 86'ed before it gained movement. In the 1965 preseason, though, the "Mel On Offense" movement started getting a groundswell of support after *Dallas Morning News* writer Gary Cartwright and *Dallas Times-Herald* Cowboys beat reporter Steve Perkins started throwing the idea around. The two often wrote about it in their papers. Letters poured in from readers wanting to see MOO. Renfro and general manager Tex Schramm secretly supported the idea, although no one ever said a word to Landry about it. Landry certainly never said anything about it to a writer.

In an exhibition game in Sacramento that year, Cartwright wrote that he suddenly heard Schramm scream: "Hey, where did he come from?"

Eyes were fixed on a new slot back in the Cowboys set: Renfro. Renfro ran a reverse on first down and lost 12 yards. On second down the reverse went the other direction for a loss of 18.

"I lived my life believing that bad things only happened to bad people."

[MEL RENFRO]

Cartwright wrote in *Confessions of a Washed-Up Sportswriter* that as he and Perkins got on the plane home, the two nodded at Landry, already in his normal seat. Landry turned his always-stoic eyes on the duo and cracked a smile.

UGLY BATTLE

In 1969, the Cowboys were practicing in North Dallas and most of the players lived in the area. Well, most of the white players. Black players were denied housing in what amounted to collusion among apartment complexes, duplexes, and housing lenders. When opponents came to town, their black players had to stay in a Ramada Inn just inside Love Field. The "there goes the neighborhood" theory was in full effect. Renfro and the other black players were forced to congregate south of the Trinity River, which separates downtown Dallas and South Dallas. It made for a lot of camaraderie, but it also meant commuting at least 25 minutes one way to practice.

In 1968, the federally mandated Fair Housing Act passed. Renfro read the legislation and wondered why it wasn't being enforced in Dallas. He went to Schramm with the idea of filing a lawsuit against a particular duplex that had denied him housing. Renfro said the team discouraged him from filing the suit. He went through with it anyway, with Schramm testifying on his behalf.

The courts eventually ruled for Renfro, issuing the first Fair Housing Act injunction in Dallas.

FINDING THE PATH

Sometimes it takes a jolt of realty to consider your own mortality. The word "cancer" has a way of doing that. It was mid-August 2002. Renfro was sitting in a doctor's office waiting word on what he thought were routine tests. He had been on a golf course in Atlantic City a few weeks back when he was told he should come in to have some minor tests. Those minor tests turned up lumps in his prostate. Two weeks later he was on an operating table to remove a tumor. "I lived my life believing that bad things only happened to bad people," Renfro told the *Ft. Worth Star-Telegram*. "So I just couldn't understand why it was happening to me. For really the first time in my life, I was scared."

So far, the cancer has not come back, even though he has to be regularly checked. The experience impacted him like nothing had in his career. He said when he found out he didn't know if would live five weeks, five years, or five minutes. "Kind of changes your perspective," Renfro said. Renfro said the cancer revelation solidified his faith and made him reassess several aspects of his life. It is an experience Renfro has been intimately familiar with.

After Renfro retired in 1977, he went through a myriad of misfortune, some brought on by his own doing, some a reflection of the lifestyle of that era's athlete.

In those days, contract negotiations normally ended with little negotiation. You got what the general manager wanted to pay. This was no carats and ice era. A lot of players gave up better paying jobs to play football because it was what they knew. There was fame, sure, but the downside was retiring with, oftentimes, little in the bank and the need for additional income. As still happens today, a lot of people took advantage of athletes, getting them involved in bad investments and leaving the athlete holding the financial bag.

Both happened to Renfro when he invested in a fried chicken franchise. The business didn't work, and Renfro had to file personal bankruptcy. The financial woes caused him to rack up back child support, leading to a couple of nights in jail. They also started Renfro on a long, winding path that eventually led him back to Dallas.

When Renfro retired, the Cowboys offered him a scouting position for $700 a month, almost a 90 percent pay cut. Renfro said he was always miffed he didn't get an assistant coaching opportunity like, among others, Mike Ditka and Dan Reeves did when they left football. Renfro left the scouting job and started a journey that took him all over the country and in and out of varied jobs. He owned a bike store and a record shop, tried selling cars, coached in the USFL, and did a stint with the St. Louis Cardinals.

In 1981, he was implicated in a Super Bowl ticket-scalping scheme. Renfro refused to take the entire blame, bringing down several others involved. He says that angered the league and probably played a part in him not being able to get a job. "My life was simply hell then," Renfro said. "Couldn't get a job, a loan to start a business. Other people with far less business experience than me went right from playing to far more lucrative jobs."

Renfro eventually landed on his feet. He started the Mel Renfro Bridge Foundation, running the foundation's community center on a ranch outside Dallas. He also took over as public relations and marketing director and as board president for the Starfish Foundation. The organization counsels drug addicts and their families. Renfro became aware of the group after former Cowboys offensive lineman Mark Tuinei died of a drug overdose. He became intimately involved after bringing his heroine-addicted niece to live with him. "I thank God for what He has given me," Renfro said. "It's been a good life. My [cancer] fears aren't there any more, but I realize that life is precious."

WAITING FOR THE CALL

Renfro was sitting in his office at Miller Beer in 1981 when Schramm called to tell him he was going to be inducted into the Ring of Honor. Renfro said he almost fell out of his chair.

It's a good thing Schramm honored Renfro, because the Ring was the closest Renfro got to the Hall of Fame until 1996, his last year of eligibility before moving to veteran status. It was an honor 15 years in the making. "I can honestly say I wasn't sure I would make the Hall of Fame," Renfro said during his acceptance speech. "Now, I've made it at the last second. I'm so very thankful."

> **"I can honestly say I wasn't sure [I would make the Hall of Fame]. Now, I've made it at the last second. I'm so very thankful."**
>
> [MEL RENFRO]

Had Renfro not been elected, the veteran's board, which inducts only one member per year, would have had to elect him. Renfro admits he was bitter he wasn't selected the first few years. After Bob Lilly and Staubach went in, Renfro figured it was simply a matter of time. Ultimately, he started to hear a familiar refrain. "I kept hearing, 'You'll make it next year, Mel,'" Renfro said, repeating the "Next Year's Champions" phrase he heard often in his playing days.

It wasn't like Renfro didn't deserve consideration. He is still the Cowboys all-time career leader in interceptions and is second in both season and career leader in kickoff return average. He is also one of the Cowboys' greatest punt returners. He was Deion Sanders before there was a Deion Sanders.

Had it not been for the lobbying of *Dallas Morning News* columnist Frank Luksa, Renfro wouldn't have made it. The Hall of Fame committee is made up of a representative from each NFL city. Those representatives make cases for players from their area. Every year for 15 years, Luksa made the Renfro case during the committee's Super Bowl week meeting. Finally, on Luksa's last year on the committee and Renfro's last on the regular ballot, Renfro got in.

Any Cowboys fan has long believed there to be an anti-Cowboys bias by Hall of Fame voters. Renfro is the only Cowboys player elected in the last 10 years. Some believe the 1969 lawsuit and the 1981 Super Bowl ticket incident were what long kept him knocking. That Drew Pearson, Cliff Harris, Charlie Waters, Ed "Too Tall" Jones, and Rayfield Wright are all still awaiting a call while players with, in some cases, inferior accomplishments are already enshrined shows Renfro may have just been a victim of the conspiracy. "Renfro [was] years late getting on the final ballot, much less approved," Luksa wrote on the day he retired from the Hall of Fame committee. "No one raised an objection about Renfro's worth, a bad sign now that I think on it, because it meant anti-Cowboy minds were fixed. So I never knew why he kept being shuffled aside. It was like fighting ghosts."

> ## "Renfro [was] years late getting on the final ballot, much less approved. No one raised an objection about Renfro's worth, a bad sign now that I think on it, because it meant anti-Cowboy minds were fixed."
>
> [FRANK LUKSA]

BOB
HAYES

Jim Shorter couldn't believe Sam Huff was serious. The Washington Redskins Hall of Fame linebacker called a blitz, and he wanted Shorter to take the "Bullet." When Shorter heard the call, he yelled back at Huff to make sure he hadn't heard what he had just heard. Yep, Huff was going to take a shot at Cowboys quarterback Don Meredith. Shorter needed to cover "Bullet" Bob Hayes one on one.

The Redskins were still arguing when they broke the huddle. Shorter telling Huff he couldn't call a blitz in that situation. Huff refusing to listen. Shorter kept on, telling him it wasn't a good idea. Finally, Huff had enough, turned to Shorter, and asked why a blitz package wouldn't work. "Because," Shorter yelled, "that means I'm covering Bob Hayes, and I can't cover Bob Hayes."

The "can't cover Bob Hayes" list is long and distinguished. It includes almost any defensive back from 1965 to 1974. "I only played against him in practice," Hayes's teammate and Hall of Famer Mel Renfro said, "but Bob Hayes was the only receiver I ever feared."

BOB HAYES

Born: December 20, 1942, in Jacksonville, Florida
Died: September 19, 2002, from prostate cancer and liver ailments
Nickname: "Bullet" and "The World's Fastest Human"
Position: Wide Receiver
Years with the Cowboys: 1965–1974
All-Pro/Pro Bowl Appearances: 4/3
Honors:
* Won two gold medals in the 1964 Tokyo Summer Olympics
* Holds or is tied for 22 franchise records
* Cowboys record: 71 career touchdown receptions
* Cowboys record: 20.0 career yards-per-catch average
* Cowboys record: 46 receptions in a rookie season
* Inducted into the Ring of Honor in 2001
* Inducted into the Pro Football Hall of Fame in 2009

Hayes was a trendsetter, one of those once-a-generation players who completely changes the way coaches approach the game. Before Hayes, football was a power game. A player lined up, knocked someone in the mouth, and hoped he was bigger and stronger than the other guy. There was no finesse. Offenses were fairly simple, and defenses were straightforward.

Then came the burner from Florida A&M. Hayes was well known before he hit Dallas. The

Cowboys drafted him in the seventh round in the 1964 draft even though he wasn't eligible to sign. Hayes spent that season training for the 1964 Tokyo Summer Olympic Games. He was on the 4x100 meter relay team and had qualified in the 100 meters. Cowboys scouting director Gil Brandt had built a reputation for finding players in far-off locales and taking chances on unconventional players. He thought if there was some way this speed demon could hold on to a football, the Cowboys might be able to overwork a team's secondary and really open things up for the running game.

Hayes eventually signed and showed up for the Cowboys' 1965 training camp. During camp, Hayes was blowing by anyone who covered him—and holding on to the ball. Brandt, Tom Landry, and most of the offense chalked Hayes's performance up to it being training camp, because he was in better shape than most because of his track schedule and the defensive backs weren't on their game yet.

One regular-season contest was all it took to convince people that Hayes was something special. The Cowboys opened the 1965 season with a 31–2 popping of the New York Giants before a record crowd at the Cotton Bowl.

On Dallas' first series, Meredith threw a pass to Hayes in the flat, much like the popular wide receiver screens in today's game. Hayes took the pass and jaunted 37 yards. On the next play he took the ball another 12 yards to set up a field goal. In the fourth quarter, Hayes showed off the big-time blazers. Meredith threw a lateral toward Hayes's shoes. Hayes scooped the ball up before it hit the ground and went 45 untouched yards for the score. "Hayes steamed by the bewildered Giants like a zephyr by a row of blue barns" is how *The Dallas Morning News* described the play the next day. In his first pro game, Hayes caught eight balls for 81 yards and a touchdown. He finished the year with a Cowboys rookie record—that still stands—of 46 receptions. The "Bullet" had arrived with a bullet.

RATTLING PASSION

Hayes grew up in Jacksonville and, despite his achievements worldwide, never strayed far from his Florida roots. He was born in 1942 when the South was segregated. When college rolled around, Hayes was good enough to have played on anyone's team. He just wasn't deemed the right color. In the early 1960s, colleges were trying to integrate. Some conferences and some states more than others. Florida stayed in the background.

Even though his speed could have sent him anywhere, Hayes wasn't eligible to go to Florida or Florida State. Instead, he went to Florida A&M, a historically black college in Tallahassee, right in Florida State's backyard. At FAMU, he set Rattlers' track records and was inducted into the school's Hall of Fame. When he moved back to Jacksonville in the mid-1990s, Hayes led a reclusive life, unless it was a FAMU event. He was a fixture at the school, especially football games. "Even after he got very sick, he still made it to the football games up here," said Eddie Jackson, a retired university vice president for public affairs and a longtime friend the day Hayes died. "We'd see he was not looking well, or feeling well, but if Florida A&M was playing, Bob Hayes would be there."

SURE WASN'T THE SHOES

Before Hayes ever played for the Cowboys, he was known worldwide as "The World's Fastest Human." It was a title well deserved after Hayes's performance in the 1964 Olympics in Tokyo.

Hayes was walking around the track preparing for his 100-meter race when he got a tap on the shoulder. The tap was from legendary sprinter Jesse Owens. He wanted Hayes to know that he and his wife were in the stands watching. He also reminded Hayes that the United States had lost the same race to the Germans four years ago. "We want it back," Owens told Hayes. Owens was concerned about Hayes's lane. Hayes was concerned about his clothing. Before Owens had approached him, Hayes had put his bag on the track's infield and begun putting

> "[I remember] Mom with tears running down her face, our flag raising ..."
>
> [BOB HAYES]

on his spikes. He got the right one on before noticing that the reason the bag had felt light while he was carrying it was because it was missing a left shoe. Hayes later found out that his roommate, boxer Joe Frazier, had knocked the shoe out of Hayes's bag and under the bed while Frazier rifled through the bag looking for gum. Hayes was now scrambling for footwear. Eventually, he found teammate Tommy Farrell who lent him a shoe. Now, Hayes would be running in a bad lane with oddly paired shoes.

It didn't matter. Hayes blasted the field, winning by seven feet and tying the world record. "[I remember] Mom with tears running down her face, our flag raising," Hayes said not long before his death in 2002. "The Emperor of Japan crossing the track. National anthem playing. The name on the billboard . . . ROBERT HAYES, USA. And me thinking, 'I'm from the world's greatest country.'"

Hayes wasn't finished representing "the world's greatest country." Proper shoes back on, Hayes anchored the 4x100-meter gold medal relay team with a performance that track experts say has yet to be equaled. He took the baton trailing by three meters. Hayes exploded down the track, passing up the French anchor and running an 8.6 split to help the United States set the world record.

IN THE ZONE

Hayes finished his rookie year with 46 catches, 1,003 yards, and 12 touchdowns, an average of 21.8 yards a catch and a touchdown every 3.8 catches. Those numbers stayed pretty steady his entire career. Hayes retired in 1975 after an uneventful year in San Francisco. During his 11 seasons, he averaged 20 yards a grab. But it was his first four years in the league that changed every team's approach on how to defend receivers and how to build their own teams. From 1965 to 1968, Hayes caught 212 balls for 45 touchdowns, an end zone celebration every 4.7 catches. The only receiver close to those numbers is Lance Alworth, who averaged a touchdown every 4.9 catches. But, Alworth played in the high-octane AFL where long bombs aimed at receivers were common and conventional thinking always went against conventional wisdom. Randy Moss (53) and Jerry Rice (49) are the only players with more receiving touchdowns in their first four years than Hayes. However, neither came close to Hayes's ability to get the ball in the end zone. Moss found pay-dirt every 5.8 catches during that time; Rice once every 5.4 grabs. "We were all a little skeptical that first training camp," Brandt said. "Then we got into the regular season, and all of the sudden he was doing the same things in those games he had in the camp."

People in Dallas also began to take notice. In the mid-1960s, the Cowboys defined close but no cigar. The team was immensely popular in the city, but some of the players were not. Meredith turned into a martyr, getting blasted early on by defensive linemen taking advantage of undersized Cowboys lines and then getting blasted later in his career by an unrelenting press and fan base. In 1965, the Cowboys started climbing the NFL ladder. Hayes was stretching defenses and bringing people to Fair Park.

Against Cleveland that year, the Cowboys drew their first sellout in the Cotton Bowl. Hayes had six catches for 84 yards including a 45-yarder he took away from two Browns at the goal line.

There were two guys in Hayes's area because *zone* was now the en vogue NFL term. Hayes had so destroyed defenses that new words and new formations were being created just for him. Every time you watch a current NFL game and hear "nickel package," "dime look," and "zone blitzes," think Hayes. "There were deep threats and then there was deep threat, Bob Hayes," said former Broncos, Giants, and Falcons coach Dan Reeves, who was a Cowboys rookie with Hayes in 1965. "Every defensive back in those days lived in fear of him. Absolutely he changed the game."

Hayes's best season was 1966, his second in the league. He had 1,232 yards on 64 catches. He was the first Cowboys receiver to go more than 1,000 yards in a season. In a 31–30 win in Washington, Hayes set a club record with 246 yards receiving, 95 of which came on one play. The mark for most yards in a game stood until a 250-yard performance by Miles Austin in 2009.

Hayes never had another season like his first two. He had 10 touchdowns in 1967 and 1968, but he had only one double-digit touchdown season (1970) in his last seven years. Despite the slide, he ended with 71 career receiving touchdowns, still a team record. Hayes also holds the Dallas mark for receiving touchdowns in a game (four). All in an era when the forward pass was treated like a necessary evil rather than a weapon.

Hayes's speed gave the Cowboys something no other team had. His impact led to sweeping, league-wide changes the likes of which are unlikely to happen again. "He wasn't just the world's fastest human," former Miami Dolphins coach Don Shula said. "He was a great athlete and football player. Put that all together, and he made you change everything on defense when you played the Cowboys."

> **"We were all a little skeptical that first training camp. Then we got into the regular season, and all of the sudden he was doing the same things in those games he had in the camp."**
>
> [GIL BRANDT]

SELF-DESTRUCTION

Bob Hayes lived as full throttle off the field as he did on it. Hayes lit up the league his first four years. Although he had good years over the last seven years of his career, he never equaled what he did early on. After he retired, Hayes admitted he started getting involved with alcohol during his Cowboys days, hitting the bottle so hard that it had a major effect on his game. "I was benched at the end of my career by Coach Landry," Hayes said in 1987. "He said I was loafing. It was very difficult for me to understand. I was giving everything. But alcohol slows you down."

Hayes was the first of a long line of high-profile Cowboys to battle drugs, alcohol, and legal problems. Hayes's issues started with alcohol but eventually led him to harder highs. He said alcoholism ran in his family. When he started drinking and it wasn't enough, he turned to drugs and that led him to cocaine. "Something in your life developed way back and you develop so many bad character defects," Hayes said in the late 1980s. "Then, all of sudden something explodes. When that happens, it is drugs and you are in jail."

All three happened to Hayes on April 6, 1978. Hayes was arrested that night in the Dallas suburb of Addison for delivering cocaine and Quaaludes to an undercover policeman. When Hayes was booked into Dallas County jail, the scene was mayhem. Jail trustees, guards, and cops jumped all over Hayes, all asking for autographs.

Hayes was eventually convicted and given a five-year sentence. He did 10 months of the term in the Texas State Penitentiary, but something about the arrest never sat well with Cowboys general manager Tex Schramm. Schramm was convinced Hayes had been set up. Although he may have been in the wrong place at the wrong time, Schramm thought Hayes was the target of a department trying to make a big-time bust. Schramm was so convinced of Hayes's innocence that he arranged with the prison to have Hayes furloughed for five days in 1979 so Hayes could attend the team's 20th anniversary celebration.

As much support as Schramm showed, he didn't let Hayes go unpunished. Schramm had already made the decision to put Hayes in the Ring of Honor during the upcoming season. Schramm stood by Hayes but felt it too early for this kind of public admiration for a man that, like it or not, had just done hard time. "Induction would have been much more difficult in the days that Bob played," Schramm said in 2000. "Players didn't get into a fraction of the trouble they do today. I didn't think it was the proper time to do it with anything that fresh."

When Hayes left prison, he tried to work his Cowboys' connections. Drew Pearson put a roof over his head. Clint Murchison and Roger Staubach both gave Hayes jobs. Staubach even paid Hayes's way through an alcohol rehab stint.

Eventually, Hayes started Person to Person, a group dedicated to educating children about drug and alcohol abuse. Hayes said that he started the group not to help the community but "for myself. It's helping me." In 1991, 12 years after he was arrested and not long after starting the group, he held a strange news conference in the same Dallas suburb to prove his innocence. Hayes said

VERNON J. BIEVER

ABOVE: Bob Hayes (22) scrambles for a warm spot during the Ice Bowl.

he had new evidence that would show he was a celebrity target and that he would be cleared if his case was heard. To give him credibility, he had Landry, then a former Cowboys coach, there.

Hayes said he was looking for a governor's pardon. He said he had copies of a sworn affidavit signed by his former codefendant that said Hayes was present at the drug swaps but never participated. Hayes said he pled guilty at the time on advice from his attorney. He said he didn't have the signed affidavits until that day and was hoping they would help clear his name. "He has struggled since losing his reputation," Landry said during the news conference. "He suffered through the years. If the governor decides to honor his request, then maybe he can get on with his life."

The governor didn't honor the request, and Hayes ended up moving back in with his parents in Jacksonville. The alcohol abuse had slowly started deteriorating his liver. Toward the end of the 1990s, every day was a fight, but it was a fight he was faring well in. He beat prostate cancer, earlier liver and kidney issues, and a heart rate that fell below 15 beats per minute, prompting a few news bulletins to declare him dead.

The "Bullet" wasn't gone yet. That happened September 18, 2002, when he finally succumbed to kidney failure at age 59 in a Jacksonville hospital. "Most of the things that happened to Bob he did to himself. He had a tremendous problem trying to overcome alcohol," former teammate Dan Reeves told *Sports Illustrated* the day of Hayes's death. "If there's anything that led to his early death, it was that . . . You try to reach out and help someone like that. It boils down to it just didn't work out."

HALL OR NOT?

Schramm got to see Hayes go into the Ring of Honor. Neither were around when the Pro Football Hall of Fame came calling in 2009.

Hayes died a year after Cowboys owner Jerry Jones put him in the Ring of Honor. Schramm missed the ceremony because he suffered broken vertebrae after a fall during the week. Schramm watched on TV as the man he already had chosen to induct over 20 years earlier finally had his name etched into the Texas Stadium wall.

Hayes likely won't be the most famous No. 22 to end up on that wall. That honor already belongs to all-time rushing king Emmitt Smith. But, for that September 2001 day, on the first weekend of games after the September 11 terrorist attacks, all was right in Cowboys land. "Bullet" Bob was finally being honored. "Ladies and gentlemen, it's overwhelming," Hayes said to a sold-out stadium. "I'm thrilled. I'm grateful. I've been blessed by the grace of God, winning two Olympic gold medals, being a world record-holder, coming to play for the world's greatest organization in the history of sports."

Even before Hayes's Ring of Honor omission was taken care of, the debate over whether Hayes belongs in the Pro Football Hall of Fame was hotly contested. His yards-per-catch and touchdowns-per-catch marks are Hall of Fame worthy. Few can say they revolutionized any sport the way Hayes did. Yet still he was not enshrined in his lifetime.

The 1978 drug distribution charge and subsequent prison term kept Hayes out of the Ring of Honor for 23 years. Those questions seemed to be answered with New York Giants linebacker Lawrence Taylor's induction. Like Hayes, New York Giants linebacker Lawrence Taylor, a Hall of Fame inductee himself, revolutionized a position but fought personal demons, including drugs.

Hayes once wrote that the arrest made him feel "like an outcast."

"There's a lot of pain in my heart because what I accomplished was second to none," Hayes wrote. "I'm not losing any sleep, but I do pay attention every year."

On the day he was inducted into the Ring of Honor, Hayes was even more direct, "When you revolutionize a part of pro football, if you're going to be fair, I [have] to be in the Ring of Honor and the Pro Football Hall of Fame. When I got to Dallas, they were averaging about 40,000 fans a game. I didn't come in here as a free agent. I came in here as a famous man, the fastest man in the world. I brought fans to the stadium. I'm not being conceited or cocky about it. I am telling the truth."

Until his dying day, Schramm agreed, "The situation with Bob Hayes and the Hall of Fame is one of the most tragic stories I've ever been associated with during my years in professional football."

VERNON J. BIEVER

ROGER STAUBACH

S teve Richardson heard the announcement and started reaching for his bags. The Cowboys' team plane would be leaving exactly an hour after the game, and everyone who was supposed to be on the plane was expected to be in his seat when that witching hour arrived.

Richardson, then a sportswriter for a Shreveport newspaper, grabbed his gear and headed out into the brutal Minnesota winter. The Cowboys were trailing the powerful Minnesota Vikings 14–10 with 36 seconds to play. There was no reason for Richardson not to step out of the baseball press box on the opposite side of the field and start heading for the locker room.

Dallas had second and 19 at the 50-yard line with defeat looking the Cowboys right in the face. Although Roger Staubach, who led 23 fourth-quarter comebacks in his career (14 in the last two minutes or overtime), was at quarterback, this was a Dallas team with 15 rookies. Minnesota had been to two straight Super Bowls, and coach Bud Grant thought this was by far his best team. Alan Page, Carl Eller, and Jim Marshall led the "Purple People Eaters" defense. Fran Tarkenton was the wily quarterback. Chuck Foreman and Ed Marinaro were the running backs that turned short Tarkenton tosses into long touchdowns. The Cowboys came in as eight-point underdogs and figured to be nothing more than roadkill for a Vikings team playing at frozen Metropolitan Stadium. Thanks to the Doomsday Defense, though, the Cowboys at least had a shot. Dallas ganged up on the Vikings' running game, figuring that Tarkenton and his receiving corps couldn't beat Cliff Harris, Mel Renfro, and the Cowboys' secondary on a consistent basis. The Vikings had only 215 net yards while Dallas ran up 356 on the famed Minnesota defense. However, the Cowboys were in a hole because their three first-half drives inside the Vikings 40-yard line produced no points.

Richardson was walking down the chilly aisle when he figured he better stop and peer around the crowd to catch a glimpse of the last play. Staubach took the snap and looked in the direction of his main man Drew Pearson. Pearson had cornerback Nate Wright one on one, and both were streaking down the field. Staubach pumped once and then chucked what would end up being the most famous pass of a famous career. Ironically, for one of the most accurate quarterbacks in NFL history the ball wasn't one of his prettiest. The ball was underthrown, causing Pearson and Wright to stop. Pearson waited for the ball to get in the area and then made a well-timed leap. There was a collision, then a battle. Then, there was Pearson strolling into the end zone with a touchdown. Dallas was up 17–14 with less than 30 seconds to play on the Vikings' home field. "I remember stopping there for just a second just so I could at least see what everyone thought was going to be the last play," said Richardson, now the executive director of the Football Writers Association of America. "I was trying to see what was going on, but from where I was I couldn't really see what all was happening. There were people every-

ROGER STAUBACH

Born: February 5, 1942, in Cincinnati, Ohio
Nickname: "Roger the Dodger" and "Captain Comeback"
Position: Quarterback
Years with the Cowboys: 1969–1979
All-Pro/Pro Bowl Appearances: 5/6
Honors:
* Five-time NFL passing champion
* Cowboys record: 83.42 all-time leading quarterback rating
* Cowboys record: 3,586 single-season passing yards in 1979
* Cowboys record: 7.67 career average yards per attempt
* Cowboys: 2nd all-time career passing yards (22,700)
* Cowboys: 8th all-time career rushing yards (2,264)
* Byron "Whizzer" White Award in 1979
* Vince Lombardi Sportsman of the Year in 1975
* Super Bowl VI Most Valuable Player
* NFL Players Association Most Valuable Player in 1971
* Heisman Trophy in 1963
* Inducted into the Ring of Honor in 1983
* Inducted into the Pro Football Hall of Fame in 1985

where yelling. I saw [Wright] fall down, and then I just heard everyone get quiet. I didn't see Pearson at first. But, when I saw that Wright had fallen down, I thought something was going on."

It had not been a good day for the Vikings. Although he didn't know it during the game, Tarkenton's dad had suffered a heart attack while watching the game and died. Now, with Pearson winning the rebounding battle with Wright, anybody wearing Vikings horns was livid. People started screaming that Pearson had interfered. Page went crazy—the future Minnesota Supreme Court judge started yelling at the officials. On the kickoff, he got an unsportsmanlike penalty and was given a free pass to the locker room for the last few plays.

Richardson knew he had to hurry to the field now. He found out a few seconds later that he needed to really pick up the pace. As he got closer to the field, he saw field judge Armen Terzian running toward the tunnel. Things were turning ugly. Bottles, oranges, and other various foreign objects started flying out of the stands. Terzian was begging the crowd to stop. Richardson said he turned to the stands to see why Terzian was waving. That's when Richardson heard the deafening silence. A whisky bottle had tagged Terzian's forehead, and the official was down for a 10 count. The bottle opened a gash across the middle of his head. "When Terzian was hit, I didn't know what else was going to go on," Richardson said. "I knew the team wasn't going to get to leave as soon as they wanted to, but they were trying to hightail it out of there as soon as possible."

> ## "When Terzian was hit, I didn't know what else was going to go on."
> [STEVE RICHARDSON]

Once Terzian got hit, Vikings fans, showing the utmost in civility, stopped littering the field. The previous week, it had been their boys on the other side when Buffalo fans threw snowballs at their players, one smacking Foreman in the face.

To this day, a Cowboys-Vikings matchup can't take place without a reference to the play that sparked a football legend. In the locker room, Staubach said the Cowboys had been all out of prayers and that that play was their last "Hail Mary." The win sent the Cowboys to Los Angeles the next week where they promptly dismissed the Rams 37–7 on their way to Super Bowl X against the Steelers.

Often forgotten in Hail Mary hoopla is the play Staubach and Pearson made earlier in the drive to even have the Hail Mary opportunity. Facing fourth and 17, Staubach hit Pearson on the sideline for 25 yards to give the Cowboys new life.

Pearson said he was just glad to get a ball his direction. Although he had just caught the crucial fourth-down pass, Pearson didn't feel Staubach had looked his way enough before the final drive.

In the book *Tom and the Boys,* Pearson said: "I was mad at Staubach and mad at Landry and mad at everybody. But, like Landry said later, when the

Cowboys needed something to happen he wanted to have Roger and me, his two big-play guys."

To this day, the play is among the most legendary for an organization that has plenty of options when it comes to great plays. Without question, it is the most famous ugly pass in Cowboys history.

"I was mad at Staubach and mad at Landry and mad at everybody. But, like Landry said later, when the Cowboys needed something to happen he wanted to have Roger and me, his two big-play guys."

[DREW PEARSON]

GUIDING THE NAVY

Much like Bob Hayes, Staubach was a household name before he joined the Cowboys as a 27-year-old rookie in 1969. As a collegian at the Naval Academy, Staubach won the 1963 Heisman Trophy and graced the covers of *Sports Illustrated* and *Time*. His celebrated college career led Navy football to the top of the polls, wins over Army, and, for him, a reputation as one of the original running-passing quarterbacks.

In a 1963 win over Southern Methodist University, Staubach became the first Midshipmen quarterback to ever rush for more than 100 yards in a game. That same season, he threw for 1,474 yards, a school record at the time. Just having a strong arm and able legs wasn't why Staubach was so hard to contain. As was the case during his NFL career, he was deadly accurate. He still holds the school record for career completion percentage, and his 1962 and 1963 seasons are still the best two seasons ever for a Navy quarterback. When Staubach was playing, there was little chance he was going to make a mistake. In 463 career attempts, he threw only 19 interceptions. He also made the most of every attempt, averaging almost 10 yards per throw in 1962 to 1963. The year he won the Heisman, he won every national region, something almost unheard of in that day of extreme regional biases and little national exposure. His margin over second-place Billy Lothridge of Georgia Tech, also a 1964 Cowboys' draft pick, is still the seventh-largest in voting history.

Staubach's combination was something that had yet to be seen at the collegiate level. The pro game still wasn't throwing the ball much, instead relying on power backs and power linemen. When Cleveland Browns quarterback Otto Graham started throwing more and opening offenses up, the NFL was forced to take notice. The observation trickled down to a Cincinnati native who got his first Navy opportunity in 1962.

Staubach started three years for the Naval Academy. The season he won the Heisman was actually his junior season. The Cowboys drafted him in the 10th round, but he wasn't even eligible to sign. He still had one more year left in Annapolis and a chance to become the first two-time Heisman winner. Injuries rattled him in 1964, and he didn't come close to the numbers he had the first two years. It didn't matter because his legendary college football status had already been sealed. And, in the last game of the 1963 season, his coming to Dallas was all but sealed.

Navy was 9–0 that year and ranked No. 2 in the nation. Staubach had led the Middies to the ever-important win over Army and Notre Dame, the last time Navy has beaten the Irish. The Midshipmen rolled into the Cotton Bowl on New Year's Day in 1964 with a chance for the national title if they could knock off No. 1 Texas. On that day, playing on a field he would step on again five years later as a pro, Staubach's arm set records, but his feet did him no favors. He left with Cotton Bowl records with 21 completions, 31 attempts, and 228 yards, a performance that got him inducted in the bowl's Hall of Fame in 2000. However, he couldn't escape the big, quick Longhorns line. Navy fell behind 21–0 in the first half. Staubach had to make space for himself in the second half by throwing on the run and trying to get outside the pass rush to make plays. When he couldn't, he would drop further back trying to find open space. Texas sacked Staubach for 47 yards in losses and held Navy to –13 yards rushing for the game.

The game ended Staubach's spectacular season, but Cowboys general manager Tex Schramm and scouting director Gil Brandt were convinced

ABOVE: Tom Landry talks things over with Roger Staubach and tight end Mike Ditka during Super Bowl VI, the Cowboys' first Super Bowl win.

that Staubach could play for them whenever he was ready. The team spent a 10th-round pick on him and told him just to continue doing what he was doing at the academy, and when the time came to talk, they would talk.

So, Staubach kept on being a man about campus. He had already played on the Navy basketball and baseball teams as a sophomore. He dropped basketball after his sophomore year to concentrate on football and baseball. The spring before winning the Heisman, he played on the Navy baseball team, serving as captain and hitting .420. After the 1964 football season, Staubach played for the College All-Stars in the annual game against the NFL champions. The All-Stars lost 24–16 in Staubach's final college game and the last football he would play for four years.

Going to the Naval Academy meant a four-year commitment to serve after his collegiate time was done. Staubach was commissioned and spent a year in Vietnam before receiving a discharge. Before he graduated, Schramm brought him to Dallas and sat him down in a hotel room. Schramm scribbled some numbers and words on a legal pad and told Staubach to sign it. It was a personal services contract that bound Staubach to the Cowboys while he was serving. Staubach would be paid, but he was expected to take part in training camps and other Cowboys functions when he was on leave. Staubach became familiar with many of the team's first players and really served as a bridge later in his career from that first group to the modern era of Tony Dorsett, Pearson, Randy White, and Danny White in the early 1980s. Staubach also grew to know Landry and his offense. Although he wouldn't play until 1969 as a 27-year-old, the Cowboys were willing to wait and willing to let Staubach continue to learn. "Staubach," Schramm told the *Dallas Morning News* the day he was drafted, "will make a nice rookie in [about] 1994."

It wasn't quite that long, but it did take a while for "Captain America" to turn into Dallas's "Captain Comeback."

MEET ME OUTSIDE

Roger Staubach was a five-time All-Pro, four-time NFL passing champion, a Super Bowl MVP, and a first-ballot Hall of Famer because he was a calm, concise tactician. He didn't show much emotion, and he certainly didn't let it cloud his judgment. In that way, he was a lot like his coach, Tom Landry. But, what the public often didn't see in either of them, was the burning intensity that made them both fierce competitors.

Before the 1974 season, the Cowboys traded for Abilene Christian quarterback Clint Longley. Longley came to Dallas with the reputation of having a big arm and an even bigger free spirit. The arm was fine with the rest of the team. It was the spirit that pushed many over the edge. Training camp in 1975 was not the year to pick on Staubach. The Cowboys had gone 8–6 in 1974 and missed the playoffs for the first time since 1965. This camp needed to be about business.

One day, Longley threw a pass in Pearson's direction. Pearson dropped the pass, and Longley was furious. As Pearson headed back to the line, Longley berated him. Staubach stepped in and said that the backup quarterback needed to step off before he got stepped over. Longley shot back at Staubach for defending Pearson, adding the barb that if he was so good at defending people, maybe there needed to be a little arrangement after practice.

The team went through the rest of their paces. Then, it was time for the main attraction. Longley and Staubach met at their designated spot and started going at it. Longley threw a glancing blow and then got taken down by the Navy veteran. Staubach was about to go into full attack mode before Dan Reeves showed up to break it up.

BELOW: Staubach, who was a whiz kid on the field, has been just as successful off of it, running his own commercial real estate firm.

ZIGY KALUZNY/GETTY IMAGES

The papers were buzzing the next day, talking about how the old man (Staubach was 33 at the time) had gotten the best of the second-year wild man. The chuckles from the writers and teammates bruised Longley more than anything Staubach had done. The day following the fight, Longley lay in wait in the locker room. As Staubach was putting on his pads, arms up, jersey hiding face, Longley put a shoulder into the first stringer knocking him backward. Staubach hit a scale and busted his head open.

Staubach went to the hospital but returned to the dorms later that day looking for another fight. Longley had left the building. He had hitched a ride to the airport and away from "The Dodger."

Longley was traded later that year, played three games the next season in San Diego, and that was it. Nine career games and one embarrassment from a legend.

SULTAN STAUBACH

With a Naval Academy education and military discipline and training, Staubach probably would have made a fortune selling ice cream on street corners had that been what he wanted to do. Staubach decided, instead, to buy up those street corners, turn them into office space, and become the head of one of the nation's most successful commercial real estate firms.

Currently, Staubach is Executive Chairman of JLL Americas, a financial and professional services firm specializing in real estate. The company serves clients in 70 countries from more than 1,000 locations worldwide, including 200 corporate offices. He got into the commercial real estate world in 1970 after his second year in Dallas. In the off seasons, he worked for Henry S. Miller, a prominent commercial firm in the area. In 1977, two years before he left the Cowboys, Staubach formed a real estate brokerage firm with Robert Holloway. Six years later, Staubach left for The Staubach Company and was on his own. Instead of simply selling properties, Staubach pioneered the "user representation" concept. His clients were people and companies looking for office and industrial space. AT&T signed on as his first national client in 1985. The next year, Staubach formed a design and construction consulting arm. This branch would oversee and consult on the actual building of the client's facility. Two years later, the company opened three new offices and Staubach was on his way to big things in other areas.

Staubach's company has represented, among others, CompUSA, GTE, Pepsi, Sun Microsystems, Toyota, Barnes & Noble, AutoNation, Shell, Mobile, Blockbuster, and Haliburton. In 1998, the company surpassed 500 employees and Staubach won *Office and Industrial Properties'* Executive of the Year honors.

The *Dallas Morning News* ranked the company as the area's 40th largest private corporation in 2004 with almost $234 million in revenue and 371 local workers and 1,141 worldwide employees. The ranking was five spots ahead of Staubach's former employer, the Dallas Cowboys. "You could never defeat Roger mentally or physically," Landry said in 1984. "He was like that in a game, in practice, or the business world."

CLIFF
HARRIS
&
CHARLIE
WATERS

Be it for thy self or for thy buddy, Charlie Waters and Cliff Harris were always looking for an edge. Sometimes, that search took the duo into the fine print of the NFL rules. "The NFL rule book says that the ground can't cause a fumble," Waters explained, "but that's not true. If a guy slips and falls down and you don't touch him, he's still live. While he's getting up, if you knock the ball out of his hands and cause a fumble then, well, the ground has a caused a fumble."

One day before a film session, Waters was waxing poetically about the intricacies of the "ground causing a fumble" rule. Harris was listening but really was just trying to get situated before preparations for "Philly Week" began. Waters wouldn't let Harris get away without giving him an assignment. "Watch how a guy gets up after he slips down," Waters said before film started rolling. "Think about it. When you fall down, at home, on the field, wherever, how do you get up? You have to put one hand down and support yourself, right? Well, if a guy is heading toward the sidelines after catching a ball and slips on the turf, he's got to put a hand down on the field to get up. That's going to expose the ball and make it a little easier to knock out."

Waters explained, however, that the strategy was going to take discipline. The natural reaction to a guy lying on the ground is to touch him so the play is dead and the player doesn't advance the ball further downfield. "Wait until the receiver starts to get up," Waters told Harris, "and then poke the ball out while

CLIFF HARRIS

Born: November 12, 1948, in Fayetteville, Arkansas
Nickname: "Captain Crash"
Position: Free Safety
Years with Cowboys: 1970–1979
All-Pro/Pro Bowl Appearances: 6/5
Honors:
* Played in five Super Bowls
* All-Pro four straight years
* Cowboys record: 4 fumble recoveries in the playoffs
* Cowboys: 2nd in fumble recoveries (tied)
* Cowboys: 3rd in punt return average for a single season (28.4 in 1971)
* NFL Alumni Legends Award (1997)
* Member of NFL All-Decade Team for the 1970s
* Inducted into the Ring of Honor in 2004

he's trying to get back on his feet. And, whoever doesn't knock the ball out, will be right there to pick the ball up and advance it."

Waters also knew Harris was going to have to resist temptation. "I knew doing this was going to be hard for Cliff," Waters said. "Anyone who ever saw Cliff Harris play knows how much of a hitter he was. And how much he liked to hit. To let a guy just lay there on the ground for a second or two before getting up was going to be hard for him."

But, Harris did wait, and the strategy did work. And it didn't take long.

A few days after throwing out his theory, the Cowboys were in Veterans Stadium tangling with the Eagles when Harold Carmichael, the man of almost 9,000 career yards and 79 career touchdowns, broke toward the sidelines early in the game for what appeared to be a routine route. He caught the pass, but slipped on the Vet's turf. Harris was trailing the play. But, instead of trying to take Carmichael's head off, Harris waited for him to get up. With one Carmichael hand on the ground and one gingerly holding the ball, Harris poked the ball out. And, true to his word, Waters scooped up the ball and ran it back to inside the Eagles' 10-yard line. Two plays later, Roger Staubach found the end zone. "The funny thing about that play," Waters said, "is that we had just talked about it that week; just a few days before actually. And, we didn't say a word to one another about it on the field. I saw Carmichael fall and saw Cliff and knew he was going to wait to go for the ball. And, that's exactly what he did."

CHARLIE WATERS

Born: September 10, 1948, in Miami, Florida
Position: Strong Safety
Years with Cowboys: 1970–1981
All-Pro/Pro Bowl Appearances: 2/3
Honors:
* Played in five Super Bowls
* Cowboys record: 9 playoff interceptions
* Cowboys record: 3 interceptions in a playoff game
* Cowboys record: 3rd in career interceptions (41)
* All-Rookie Team (1970)
* Cowboys Silver Anniversary Team
* Inducted into the South Carolina Hall of Fame
* Inducted into the Clemson Hall of Fame

I FEEL YOU, MAN

For as much as Dallas' Doomsday Defense was known for its front seven, the secondary may have been the most vital cog in the smooth-running engine. The safety tandem of Waters and Harris were the leaders of a unit that provided the perfect complement to the speedy, overpowering presence of Randy White, Harvey Martin, Ed "Too Tall" Jones, Bob Breunig, and company.

Take Waters and Harris away from one another and both likely would have been good NFL players. Put them together and the Cowboys had one of the headiest and productive defensive backfield tandems ever. They were similar players with differing backgrounds. But, on the field together, something special happened. The two had that "something" that is an enduring quest for any team in any sport. They had the kind of chemistry that can't be scouted and can't be drafted. It can only be fostered and molded from years of playing alongside one another and from knowing the other guy like you know yourself. That knowledge of each other is what made the Waters-Harris combination so successful. And, the two made so many plays by playing off one another that, at times, the stories simply run together. "You have to remember that when we tell stories," Waters said, "they are our versions of the stories, because it did seem like one of us was always making a play because of what the other one did, and [it] didn't matter what the opponent was doing or who the opponent was. Cliff and I knew that if we did what we said we were going to do, opportunities were going to be available."

On this particular play, Harris knew Waters was going to be available even if he couldn't see him. Waters still remembers the play vividly.

Waters said he remembers seeing the receiver break for the sidelines with Harris right behind him. Instead of going for a bone-crushing hit, Harris backed off, picked off the pass, and started heading the opposite direction. He made his way to just inside the 10-yard line before encountering resistance. But Harris was determined to get this ball in the end zone. He had just given up a jarring highlight-reel hit. This thing was going in for six. He just needed help from his buddy.

Harris didn't turn to see whether Waters was trailing the play; he knew Waters was there. Harris pitched the ball behind him as he was hit. Waters scooped up the ball and walked into the end zone. After the game, Waters asked Harris how he knew Waters would be trailing him instead of blocking for him. Harris had a simple one-word answer, "Brainwaves."

UNIQUE PATHS, SAME DESTINATION

One played in the Division I big time. The other in the Arkansas backwoods. One was Dallas' third-round pick in the 1970 draft. The other was rolling around the dusty sandlots of the semi-pro circuit when the Cowboys called.

Waters was a homegrown product, the kind of in-state star with the storybook good looks Clemson dreamed of snagging. When he got to Death Valley in 1967, he wowed all on both sides of the ball, just like he had done at North Augusta High School. In addition to playing defense, Waters caught more than 22 passes per year. Coaches put Waters on offense because his speed was game-breaking. He was an All-ACC pick his senior year and ended his career with a 17.1 yards-per-catch average, a mark that is still among the school's best.

Harris rolled up accolades while at NAIA Ouachita Baptist University in Arkadelphia, Arkansas. Although the Cowboys were genius at snagging small-school talent, Gil Brandt and his wagon didn't make its way through Arkadelphia until Harris had paid semi-pro dues. Even then, Harris only got a free-agent contract and an invitation to camp. It was at that same camp where the golden boy from South Carolina also showed up.

LOCKDOWN MODE

Dallas had never played in the Super Bowl before Harris and Waters came on board in 1970. Along with names such as Staubach, Randy White, Ed "Too Tall" Jones, and, eventually, Tony Dorsett, Waters and Harris were part of a nucleus that went to five of the next nine Super Bowls, winning twice.

ABOVE: The hard-hitting Cliff Harris (43) and the smooth, heady Waters formed one of the most dominant safety tandems in NFL history.

Staubach was Dallas' face, but "America's Team" was defined by the Doomsday Defense.

In the 10 years Cliff and Charlie played in the Cowboys' secondary, the team went to the playoffs nine times. However, the duo didn't just arrive in Texas and grab starting spots. Harris broke in first, grabbing the free safety spot during training camp his first year. But because he was in the reserves and was summoned for Vietnam duty, Harris trained with his military unit during the week but still played for the Cowboys on the weekends. However, he wasn't the starter at free safety. That gig went to Waters. Harris got the spot back next year. However, Waters had played so well that Landry had to find a place for him. Landry moved Waters to cornerback, but it wasn't until 1975 when Landry put Waters at strong safety that Waters and Harris simply became "Cliff and Charlie."

For the next four seasons, the two handled the middle of the Doomsday Defense. Both were run stoppers and devastating hitters and had instincts around the ball. Knowing Harris, who Waters said was one of the most vicious and feared hitters in NFL history ("Neither Ronnie Lott nor Jack Tatum had anything on Cliff Harris when it came to knocking players out of games,"

ABOVE: Waters (41), among the team's all-time leaders in interceptions, was, like Harris, a solid special teams contributor.

Waters said.), and Waters were patrolling the middle and pushing things to the sidelines allowed the linebackers and defensive line to be more aggressive. Having Cliff and Charlie on board even affected the way the Cowboys drafted, allowing the team to go after athletes and turn them into dominating defensive linemen and linebackers. Cliff and Charlie would take care of pass coverage. Linebackers and defensive linemen only had to worry about stopping the run and getting to the passer.

Harris is one of the best undrafted free agents ever. The guy from small-school Arkansas changed offensive game planning in the 1970s. Teams had to know where Harris was, or a receiver was going to get his head taken off or a quarterback was going to get picked, as happened 29 times in Harris's career. In 10 seasons, "Captain Crunch" went to six Pro Bowls, was first-team All-NFL four straight seasons, and made the 1970s Team of the Decade.

> **"I could have kissed Charlie right then and there."**
>
> [CLIFF HARRIS]

Once he found his strong safety home, Waters made the Pro Bowl trip three times, twice with Harris, and three All-Pro teams. Waters's 41 career interceptions still rank among the top five in Cowboys history.

The bigger the game, the better the duo played. In 1976, Dallas was fighting St. Louis for a divisional title and playoff berth when the two got together at Texas Stadium on Thanksgiving Day. With less than two minutes to play and the Cowboys nursing a five-point lead, quarterback Jim Hart drove the Cardinals deep into Dallas territory. Four times Hart went to the end zone for six. Each time he came up empty, courtesy of either Harris or Waters or both. The Cowboys avenged an earlier loss to St. Louis and escaped a 19–14 win. Waters also escaped an embarrassing thank-you from his teammate.

On Hart's first pass, Harris slipped, allowing St. Louis tight end, J.V. Cain, to roam freely. Waters was covering Mel Gray, but he rushed over to help his buddy when he saw Hart about to release. Waters dived and tipped the ball enough to keep it away from Cain. "I could have kissed Charlie right then and there," Harris said after the game.

In the playoffs, the duo pushed the bar even higher. Waters still holds the Cowboys' postseason record with nine career interceptions, three coming against the Chicago Bears in 1977.

Dallas' two Super Bowl wins in the Cliff and Charlie era came courtesy of the Doomsday Defense. In Super Bowl VI, the Cowboys held Miami, which won the next two Super Bowls, from reaching the end zone, the only time a team has failed to score a touchdown in Super Bowl history. In Super Bowl XII, Waters and Harris led a unit that harassed Denver into four interceptions on 8–25 passing.

Injuries eventually got the best of the duo. Waters missed the 1979 season with a knee injury, the same year Harris retired. Waters played two more seasons, made another Pro Bowl, and came close to a sixth Super Bowl appearance after the 1981 season before Joe Montana found Dwight Clark in the back of the Candlestick Park end zone on a dreary San Francisco afternoon.

Not long after, Waters joined Harris in retirement.

SNUBS HURT

One of the great debates among Cowboys' old timers is whether or not a Cowboys bias exists when it comes to Hall of Fame balloting. Especially when it comes to Cowboys versus Pittsburgh Steelers. The two teams of the 1970s played in Super Bowls X and XII, with Dallas taking it on the chin twice.

Nineteen players from those teams are in the Hall, seven from Dallas, 12 from Pittsburgh. Both Cowboys-Steelers games are considered among the greatest Super Bowls ever. However, Harris, who played a major role in both, is not among the 19. In May 2004, after

> **"There you sit in admiration of what the athletes are doing, but you want to be out there competing with them. I don't want to be a participant. I want to win it."**
>
> [CLIFF HARRIS]

20 years of being overlooked, Harris had finally had enough. "What was really disappointing was that none of the three Cowboys—myself, [offensive tackle] Rayfield Wright, and [wide receiver] Bob Hayes—made it to the Hall of Fame," Harris told an assembled group at his charity golf tournament in Hot Springs, Arkansas. "I will have to say I'm much more disappointed than I expected."

Much of the perception that the Steelers dominated the Cowboys during the 1970s came because of one rare time when Harris didn't get his man. In Super Bowl X, Harris came off the edge and drilled Terry Bradshaw. However, Bradshaw got enough on a pass to get the ball in Lynn Swann's general direction. Swann tipped the ball and made a juggling 53-yard catch to set up the go-ahead score in the Steelers' 21–17 win. Three years later, Pittsburgh got the best of Dallas 35–31. "Super Bowl XIII, as it turned out, was one of the games, from the perspective of that decade, that influenced things," Harris said that day. "All people remember is Super Bowl XIII."

This 2004 vote particularly hurt because Harris, after a major urging from Dallas media, made it to the final 15. Only John Elway and Barry Sanders made it on the regular ballot. The veterans committee passed over Harris, Hayes, and Wright for Minnesota Vikings defensive lineman Carl Eller and Philadelphia Eagles offensive lineman Bob Brown. "When I first made it to the final 15, I felt that was a goal in itself. But when I didn't make it, I felt like I was watching the Olympics in the stands," he said. "There you sit in admiration of what the athletes are doing, but you want to be out there competing with them. I don't want to be a participant. I want to win it."

KEEPING IT TOGETHER

Harris jumped from one Texas tradition (football) to another (the oil business) in the early 1980s. He did well on two fronts. He made his cash when the industry was booming and was smart enough to get out of the business before it busted.

In 1995, with electricity deregulation on the horizon, Harris jumped in with partners Kelcy Warren and Ray Davis to found Energy Transfer Group, an electricity supplier company. The group buys electricity from larger suppliers and sells it to smaller municipalities and cooperatives. Steadily, the company grew and, in 1999, branched out to an Internet telecommunications group, where Harris focuses most of his time.

Waters and Harris resumed their partnership in 1996 when Harris brought Waters to Energy Transfer Group to work in sales. Most of Harris's old co-op duties have fallen to Waters, whose return to Dallas was a circuitous one. Waters joined the CBS broadcast booth after retiring, before settling on the NFL sidelines as a Denver Broncos assistant under former Cowboy Dan Reeves. Waters began his coaching career as a special teams coach and ended it as Wade Phillips's defensive coordinator. Waters also roamed the college sidelines, coordinating an Oregon Ducks defense that played in the Cotton Bowl after the 1995 season.

Now it's Cliff and Charlie living it up together. The way it's been for years. The way it is supposed to be.

AP/WWP

THOMAS
"HOLLYWOOD"
HENDERSON

Thomas Henderson isn't one of the best players in Cowboys history. But "Hollywood" Henderson is the team's greatest story. There is no ideal place to start with "Hollywood" because every story is good. And every story is full throttle. Although he was only in Dallas five seasons, no one did more living in five years than Henderson.

There is the story about "Hollywood" and his love affair with his calf-length beaver coat. His trash talking and self-promoting were legendary. He was a linebacker who returned kicks.

There is the story about him knocking Vikings running back Chuck Foreman in the mouth, falling down, and tipping a Fran Tarkenton pass up in the air and then grabbing his own tip for an interception—all in his first pro start.

Even his off-field actions, full of debauchery and degradation—including an arrest in California that led to jail time—match his leaning toward spectacle and controversy.

Then, there is the Thomas Henderson turnaround story. The one that starts with him going through a 12-step program before he goes to prison. The one that has seen him stay clean since 1983. The one that has him intimately involved in the East Austin community where he grew up. The one that ends with him taking home $10 million in the Texas lottery in March 2000 and finally having his life come full circle.

GOING THE DISTANCE

"Hollywood" wasn't "Hollywood" when the Cowboys made Thomas Henderson the 18th overall pick in the 1975 draft. That year's haul, dubbed "The Dirty Dozen," is one of the most productive in Dallas history. The Cowboys pulled in 12 players that made the roster, including Randy White and Henderson in the first round and fellow Doomsday linebacker Bob Breunig in the third round.

Henderson had made a name for himself at Langston University by being a playmaking linebacker whose build wasn't stereotypical for the position. At 6-foot-2 and 221 pounds, his size was ideal linebacker, but his speed was not. He was one of the fastest and most athletic players on the team in addition to being one of the strongest. Playing at a small-college level, Henderson dominated on talent alone. He didn't have to spend hours in the

THOMAS HENDERSON

Born: March 1, 1953, in Austin, Texas
Nickname: "Hollywood"
Position: Linebacker
Years with Cowboys: 1975–1979
All-Pro/Pro Bowl Appearances: 0/1
Honors:
* Played in three Super Bowls
* Cowboys: Top 10 longest kickoff return (97 yards in 1975)
* Cowboys: Top 10 longest interception return (79 yards in 1977)
* Won Texas Lottery on March 24, 2000

weight and film rooms in order to be an All-American. Even though he played in a lower division, NFL people were fairly familiar with Henderson. The Cowboys, however, were especially familiar with the Austin native and with his performance.

Despite the old-fashioned appearance and approach, Landry was ahead of his time both with schemes and in ways to build offense and defenses. In the mid-1960s, scouting director Gil Brandt began to provide Landry with players with overall athletic ability that could be molded into the Cowboys' needs. During that time, Landry hired the league's first strength and conditioning coach as well as a former college track coach to make players bigger and faster; thus, as Landry loved to do, creating mismatches in one area that allowed other positions to make plays.

In 1965, Dallas drafted Jethro Pugh out of tiny Elizabeth City State because he was 6-foot-7 and 260 pounds and had decent speed. With the newly hired coaches, Landry figured he could turn someone of that size into a playmaking defensive end. Pugh ended up being one of the stalwarts of the defense in the late 1960s, and his success led Brandt and general manager Tex Schramm to look for opportunities to take the same kind of overlooked player.

The success also led Dallas to think the philosophy could work in other positions. In 1975, the Cowboys grabbed the playmaking Henderson.

In training camp, Henderson showed he was even faster than they had thought, especially when compared to the other linebackers. At the time, Lee Roy Jordan was still patrolling the middle and was very much the leader of the defense. However, Henderson's speed and explosiveness around the ball intrigued Landry. He didn't think Henderson was going to be a fit immediately as a starter. But Landry thought if he could get Henderson around the ball in different ways, he could give the Cowboys an advantage.

One of those ways was on special teams. Although he was a linebacker, Landry felt Henderson and his speed could make plays in the kicking game. Always looking to exploit an opportunity and the element of surprise, Landry decided Henderson would be a part of a new reverse play on kickoff returns. In the second game of Henderson's 1975 rookie season, all the maneuvering and wondering how to get Henderson on the field paid off.

After St. Louis scored to cut Dallas' lead to 21–17 with just over two minutes left in the third quarter, the Cardinals kicked off to defensive back Rollie Woolsey. Woolsey ran to one side and started looking for his fellow rookie. Henderson began running in the opposite direction toward Woolsey. Woolsey handed the ball to the big linebacker at the three-yard line and started watching. Henderson now had the kickoff and was going opposite the play flow with a couple of blockers, including White, ahead of him. He followed his openings, made a couple of moves, and turned on the jets.

The Cardinals, Cowboys, and the rest of the NFL found out 97 yards later when Henderson was in the end zone dunking the ball over the goalpost, Dallas had found another athlete that might redefine how a position is played and how a player is used.

Henderson returned three more kicks that season, averaging only 11 yards-per-return. He had only one career return afterward, an eight-yarder two years later. However, the 97-yard return still ranks among the top seven longest returns in Cowboys history and is the third longest ever by a rookie. The play also convinced Landry he needed to get this rookie from Langston on the field a little more.

Henderson's touchdown gave the Cowboys a 28–17 lead, a 2–0 start, and the confidence that this young, supposedly rebuilding team could win. That team ended up winning the NFC East, upsetting the highly favored Minnesota Vikings in the "Hail Mary" game and playing the Pittsburgh Steelers in the Super Bowl.

"Hollywood" had just arrived.

HOLLYWOOD-SIZED TALENT

Henderson caused Landry so much frustration because Henderson sometimes looked like the Pro Bowl linebacker he was. Landry put up with the ups and downs in Henderson's on-field performance, and his off-field distractions, because when "Hollywood" came to play, there weren't many who could change a game like he could.

Among the great Cowboys teams of the 1970s, the 1977 team that went 15–2 and beat Denver in the Super Bowl is considered the best. It was the perfect combination of precision offense and dominating defense. It was also the first year Henderson stepped into a starting spot.

In his first game as a starter, he helped inflict even more damage on the Minnesota Vikings, stalling a drive with a crushing hit on fullback Chuck Foreman and then intercepting the tipped pass. Two weeks later, in the third game of an eight-game winning streak to open the season, it was the "Hollywood" Henderson Show against the Tampa Bay Buccaneers at Texas Stadium.

Early in the first quarter, Tampa Bay tight end Bob Moore met Henderson after catching a pass. "Hollywood" rattled Moore's cage and sent him to the sidelines for the rest of the afternoon with a sprained knee. Later in the period, Henderson intercepted the first pass of his career and, like anything "Hollywood" did, turned it into a spectacle.

On first down from the Dallas 27-yard line, Buccaneers quarterback Gary Huff threw a short pass into the flat for Moore's replacement, Dana Nafziger. Henderson read the play perfectly, jumped out to meet Nafziger, and stepped in front of the pass. He picked the ball off and started rumbling down the sidelines. He got a nice courtesy block from Harvey Martin, but, in the open field, no one was catching "Hollywood." Seventy-nine yards later, Henderson was in the end zone, once again, dunking the ball over the goalpost.

The return still ranks among the top 10 longest interception returns in Cowboys history and, at the time, was the team's longest in 12 years. When Henderson later knocked prized Tampa Bay running back Ricky Bell out of the game, the spectacle was complete. "A gratifying afternoon," Henderson said after the game.

WELL, YOU'RE SO DUMB…

Thomas Henderson was just being "Hollywood" and he was taking the act to South Florida. In January 1976, Dallas and Pittsburgh had met in the same locale. In that game, Lynn Swann set a Super Bowl record for receiving yards, and the Steelers broke Cowboys fans' hearts with an interception on the last play of the game to preserve a 21–17 win.

It was 1979, and again, Dallas and Pittsburgh were in the Super Bowl in Miami. The Cowboys were in their third Super Bowl in four years. The year before, Dallas rolled over Denver in New Orleans for the organization's second title. This time, the Cowboys strolled into Miami on an eight-game winning streak and two weeks removed from pasting Atlanta, 28–0, in the NFC Championship Game. As if "Hollywood" Henderson needed any more confidence, in the NFC Championship win he had forced a fumble and returned an interception 68 yards for a touchdown. Throw in God knows what else, and high-octane "Hollywood" was about to make an appearance.

During an interview session, talk turned to the Steelers' Louisiana-bred quarterback Terry Bradshaw, who was sharing cover duties on the week's *Newsweek* with Henderson. Bradshaw had torn up the AFC that year. It was the first year defenders weren't allowed to make contact with receivers more than five yards downfield. The more restrictive rules meant offense was going to play a much bigger role. Bradshaw did just fine, throwing 28 touchdown passes and winning Player of the Year honors. Still, there was a stereotype that, because of his back-porch accent and sometime penchant for being stubborn (Bradshaw once called a sweep on third and 30 and almost got punched in the huddle), he wasn't the sharpest knife in the drawer.

That was all the ammunition "Hollywood" needed. As reporters gathered around the quote machine, Henderson delivered one for all time when asked about the man he would be chasing come Sunday. "Bradshaw?" Henderson quipped. "He is so dumb he couldn't spell 'cat' if you spotted him the 'c' and the 'a.'"

> # "[Terry Bradshaw] is so dumb he couldn't spell 'cat' if you spotted him the 'c' and the 'a.'"
> [THOMAS HENDERSON]

The quote immediately made its way to the Pittsburgh side of the field. The Steelers had won Super Bowls IX and X with Bradshaw at the helm. He had established himself as one of the best players in the league. And, with one five-second sound bite all of the old Bradshaw stereotypes were back. "We had a great season [14–2], I played better than I had played my whole life, and it was like 'So what?'" Bradshaw said 20 years later. "[Henderson] makes a comment, and all of a sudden people are writing 'Terry's a dummy' again. It was like, 'What do I have to do to prove myself?'"

Several Steelers players said that even during the game the quote wasn't forgotten. Henderson and Bradshaw crossed paths several times, once when Henderson crushed Bradshaw causing a fumble and leading to a 37-yard Mike Hegman touchdown return.

But Bradshaw got the next and last laugh. In the fourth quarter, a penalty was called on Bradshaw for a delay of game, but Henderson never stopped pursuing his prey. Although the play had been blown dead, Henderson kept going, grabbing Bradshaw and throwing him to the turf. Steelers running back Franco Harris saw the whole incident and was livid. The two jawed a bit with Harris telling "Hollywood" he would get plenty of him in a bit. The next play was a trap play that ran right through the heart of the Cowboys' defense. Harris blasted through the hole and took it to the house from 22 yards out. "I was kind of upset at what Henderson was doing," Harris said after the game. "It was after the whistle had blown, and he just kept coming. That kind of defense is uncalled for."

The score put Pittsburgh up 28–17 en route to an eventual 35–31 win. Bradshaw threw four touchdowns and was named MVP.

But, the Steelers weren't done getting back at "Hollywood." After a Cowboys score, Henderson walked onto the field for the kickoff, where he met Pittsburgh's Hall of Fame defensive lineman Mean Joe Greene. "Hey," Greene asked, "what's a superstar like you doing on the kickoff team?"

Pittsburgh got the victory, but the quotes are some of the all-time great Super Bowl moments. Bradshaw said Henderson's line bothered him for a long time because of what all he had gone through to get to that moment. Even though Bradshaw won the Super Bowl MVP the next year as well, the backwoods stereotype stayed with him. Although he has made a lot of money on FOX with that personality, it wasn't something he really wanted to embrace at the time.

Before the 1999 Super Bowl, 20 years after the quote, Bradshaw sat down with Henderson for a one-on-one interview for the FOX pregame show. The two played nice and, Henderson said, made amends. "I had no idea that my statement affected him so much," Henderson told DallasNews.com. "I was just trying to hype the game."

YOU'RE FIRED

Landry had had enough of "Hollywood" Henderson creating emergencies for him. This straw didn't just break the camel's back. It sent the camel to its knees and then kicked him while he was down.

The Cowboys were in a fierce battle with Washington and Philadelphia for the 1979 Eastern Division title. Dallas marched into RFK Stadium with a

RIGHT: Thomas "Hollywood" Henderson celebrates after making a stop in Super Bowl XIII. Henderson made himself famous with his legendary quote about Steelers quarterback Terry Bradshaw.

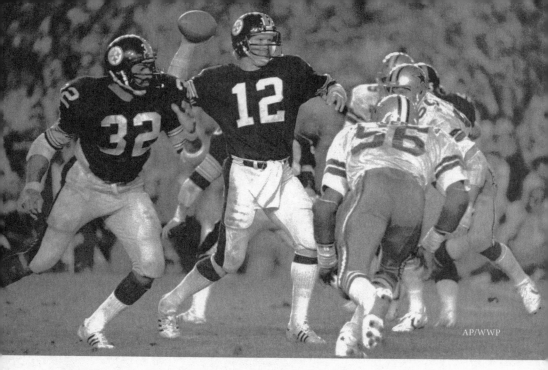

AP/WWP

ABOVE: In Super Bowl XIII, Steelers quarterback Terry Bradshaw (12) and Henderson (56) were involved in one of the NFL's most famous trash-talking incidents. Bradshaw's play proved bigger than Henderson's words.

one-game lead. They left the nation's capital having lost two of three, in a three-way tie, and toting an about-to-be-canned linebacker.

As the final ticks rolled off a 34–20 Redskins victory, Henderson roamed the sidelines looking for someone to put his face on TV. He found a taker and began hamming it up for the folks at home while his teammates were getting blasted just a few feet away. Coaches hollered at him; other players got in his face. "Hollywood" returned the favor. Anyone who dared cross into Henderson's turf best be ready to face the consequences. The same went for Landry as Henderson found out the next morning.

With little fanfare, Henderson showed up to work and was told he needed to hit the bricks. He was no longer on the team. He had been fired. And, it mattered none to him.

With countless reporters gathered around his ride and hanging on anything "Hollywood," Henderson laughed about the situation, saying he would be just fine in this world. Then, he uttered one of his most famous lines: "I'm tall, talented, neat in the waist, cute in the face, and they call me 'Hollywood.' How can I lose?"

The firing came just days before the Cowboys' Thanksgiving Day game against Houston. Dallas lost 30–24, the team's third loss in a row. At first, reporters weren't aware why one of Dallas' most productive linebackers wasn't around. The papers first reported that "Hollywood" had "retired." In effect he did. He never played another down. ". . . [T]he Cowboys told me the team knew of my cocaine use and underworld friends," Henderson wrote in an open letter to the city in 1997 that appeared in the *Dallas Morning News*. "As I walked to my car, I had this overwhelming feeling of powerlessness."

"Thomas Henderson was such a showman," Landry said in a 1989 interview. "I couldn't tell whether or not he was serious. He was another great talent wasted."

CRASHING DOWN

"Hollywood" Henderson was so wild that some of his tales are hard to believe. Henderson rode Dallas as hard as it could be ridden during his time. He says during the heyday of the 1970s in Big D he "had the run of the city" and lived the wild life with celebrities such as Marvin Gaye and Richard Pryor. There were stories of dancers, drugs, big-time dollars, and cops on his side. When "Hollywood" was patrolling Dallas, it was his world and everyone else was just living in it. "The one thing I learned most was I wasn't black," Henderson told the *Dallas Morning News* in a 1987 interview in which he made his most outrageous claims. "I was gray and silver. And I got away with a lot of things in Dallas being under that protective umbrella of the system of the management that was highly connected to the police department."

Henderson said he had a drug problem before the team took him in 1975. He said he went to the team about it. The Cowboys, at the time, denied any knowledge of the problem. While he was on the team, his drug use escalated. Henderson said he smoked marijuana every day. If the team had a few off days in a row, he would use harder drugs. At one point, he said he was spending $1,200 a day to feed his addiction. He would go to the gentlemen's clubs and just start running the place. He said it was all part of being a Dallas Cowboy during that time. "Take the success, the exposure, coupled with cocaine use on a daily basis . . . throw it all in a basket and you come up with Thomas Henderson."

Henderson said a lot of his problems came from simply not knowing how to handle what had been handed to him. When he got his first big-time football cash, Henderson said his biggest decision was what car and stereo system to buy.

After the Cowboys let him go in 1979, no other team wanted to sign him. So Henderson tried to see if "Hollywood" played in Hollywood. He didn't have much luck finding work, but with his addiction he fit right in to the California drug scene. On November 2, 1983, being "Hollywood" caught up with Thomas Henderson. He was arrested in Long Beach, California, for drug possession, and there were allegations of indecent activity with a minor. Henderson was sentenced to four years and eight months; he served two years of the sentence.

But before he began his serving his sentence, Henderson's life started turning around. He went into a 12-step recovery program that he says changed his life. He did his prison term clean and is now a motivational speaker discussing his turbulent experience.

RING IT UP

In the age of eBay, being able to get a piece of your hero's jewelry is much easier than it used to be. Of course, when you rack up back taxes and the government comes knocking at your door demanding your Super Bowl ring, putting the pieces up for auction isn't really a choice.

The IRS seized Henderson's Super Bowl XII ring in 1984 to pay back taxes while he was in a California prison. Henderson was no stranger to losing rings, having left his 1978 NFL Championship ring in a rehab center in the early 1980s.

He has never tried to track that ring down, but he did want his Super Bowl ring back. The same year Uncle Sam took possession, a Cowboys fan in West Texas bought the ring for $11,000, even though the same fan said in an interview that year that "it would have been better had this been Charlie Waters's, but this will do."

When he got out of jail, Henderson tracked the fan down. The fan promised to give the ring back one day, but never got the chance because he was killed in a car wreck just weeks after making the agreement with Henderson. The fan's family demanded money from Henderson. "Hollywood" refused to buy something he felt he had earned by playing his guts out on the field.

A few years later, while on a date, the woman he was eating with told Henderson to look under his napkin. Staring him in the face was a different kind of ice. The kind of ice worth thousands to collectors and fans, but priceless to the one who earned it.

I'M SORRY

It took a long time before Thomas Henderson was able to come clean about his actions. Sure, he had been clean since 1983, had made several self-help films, talked to countless kids, made numerous speeches, and built a nice motivational empire. But he had never talked so publicly about his past as he did when he wrote a piece for the *Dallas Morning News* with the headline "DEAR DALLAS." The open letter to the city appeared in the Sunday, January 5, 1997, edition and laid out all of the details of the 1983 arrest. Henderson admitted he went "paranoid nuts smoking crack." He said he wanted to quit but didn't know how. This letter was the first time Henderson had ever given a detailed account of what went on that night. He wrote that it was cathartic. "For closure and my own esteem, I had to share this with you."

Henderson wrote that he had taken the proper steps to become and stay sober. He apologized to the city as a whole and said he was thankful a sober lifestyle was giving him a new life lease and a new outlook. He let readers know that admitting his mistakes was therapeutic, and that if "Hollywood" could go clean anyone can. He closed by thanking God for letting him smile again. "But please God," he wrote, "don't ever let me forget that I cried."

JACKPOT, BABY!

He had gone to the same store every day for the last 10 years. He figured he had spent about $30,000 over that time trying to do just like any other person who plays the numbers every Wednesday and Saturday. This time, "Hollywood" just didn't play. He won.

On March 24, 2000, Thomas Henderson went from a nice, comfortable lifestyle in the Texas Hill Country to major Texas millionaire when he won a $28 million jackpot in the Texas lottery. "I always knew I was going to win it sometime," Henderson said not long after winning.

The winning numbers (5, 8, 17, 35, 38, and 41) were a computer generated "quick pick." The cashier at Nau's, where "Hollywood" still buys his tickets, said Henderson bought $100 worth of tickets that night. Despite 60,000,000-to-1 odds, Henderson cashed in, taking home a lump sum of around $10 million after taxes.

Henderson has since used the money to build a stadium in East Austin with an eight-lane track. The stadium and track are part of his East Side Youth Services and Street Outreach program. He had raised $250,000 in 1997 for the facility by going on a hunger strike.

With the cash from the lottery, Henderson, who said he was worth "a couple million" through his motivational tapes, doesn't have to worry about missing meals.

To celebrate, he chose a sausage and egg biscuit, milk, and powdered doughnuts. He admitted at the time, though, that had the jackpot happened in a different era the celebration would "have been laced with some cocaine and alcohol and the whole insanity."

Instead, he bought his mom a Town Car, took care of his kids, and retired to the good life. "I do nothing," Henderson said. "And I don't start that until about noon."

ED
"TOO TALL"
JONES

I f only "Too Tall" had been just a tad taller. If only he'd jumped just a bit higher. Then, maybe, he would have been able to knock the ball down. He would have been able to keep one of the biggest gut-kicking plays in league history off NFL Films forever.

It didn't matter your age. From seven to 70, if you rooted for the silver and blue star, January 10, 1982, might has well have been football Armageddon. That was the day Joe Montana rolled right and then tossed it to Dwight Clark, who promptly slammed it to the ground and laughed in Cowboys fans' faces as they watched the beginning of their team's decade-long decline toward near death.

The 1981 NFC Championship Game was one of those pendulum-swinging games. The Cowboys rolled into Candlestick Park with a dominance that didn't take off when the calendar flipped to the 1980s. San Francisco was an upstart team with a 25-year-old Montana, a third-round pick, leading the way for Bill Walsh's West Coast offense. The Cowboys still had almost everyone in place from the heyday. After walking over Tampa Bay 38–0 at Texas Stadium in the divisional playoff, beating the young 49ers almost seemed like a formality. The silver and blue in the Silverdome playing the Super Bowl. It just seemed so perfect.

Then came the pass that never was supposed to be. It was 27–21 Cowboys, and all Dallas needed was for its "D" to come up big. San Francisco took over at their 11-yard line. Coach Tom Landry and defensive coordinator Ernie Stautner took out the linebackers and went with the nickel package. Instead of panicking with the pass, Walsh kept the ball on the ground. Levil Elliott picked up 30 yards on three carries. Freddie Solomon got a first down on a reverse. Steadily, the 49ers were moving. With every run and short throw, Montana was becoming more confident. With 58 seconds left, it was, again, third and three, this time only six yards from paydirt. Walsh called timeout and called third- and fourth-down plays. Landry put D.D. Lewis and the rest of the linebackers back in. Sensing Montana was about to roll out, "Too Tall" called a stunt with himself and Larry Bethea. Walsh, meanwhile, told Montana to hit a streaking Solomon coming over the middle. Instead, Montana rolled right, fired, and found Clark to give the 49ers a 28–27 lead.

Had the up-front stunt against Montana been run right, there would likely have been no Clark catch. There would have been no space for Montana to improvise and no chance for him to throw a ball that most thought he was just trying to get rid of.

On the play, Jones was going to go inside from his end spot and Bethea would go from tackle to the outside and defend against anything on the edge. If Jones didn't make the play, Bethea would be right there for the sack. "I'd set up my man for an inside move," Jones told the *Dallas Morning News* on the 10th anniversary of The Catch. "If I could get [Montana] out, if I couldn't sack him, I'd force him into [Bethea]. I made a perfect call . . . I thought. I beat my man. Montana recognized my jersey wasn't one of his and made a move outside. A perfect play for Bethea if he'd made the stunt. He didn't."

Instead, there is the famous shot of Lewis and "Too Tall" trying to run down Montana while the wily quarterback was about to chalk up his first of many legends. Because of Jones's 6-foot-9 frame and outstretched arms, Montana threw a high floater that hung in the air. "He had to put this big arc on it to keep me from batting it down," Jones said.

That caused Everson Walls, who was defending Clark, to think Montana was throwing to some guy in the fifth row. Jones said that had Montana not been throwing the ball away he would have tried to plant and throw a strike to the back of the end zone. Had he tried that, Jones said his long arms would have gotten to the ball.

Clark maintains to this day that the play was something the team practiced and that it was a designed play. Drew Pearson said he saw Montana on the memorabilia circuit not long after The Catch, and Montana admitted he was simply trying to live another day. Jones heard Montana tell the same story not long after at the Pro Bowl.

The loss was a devastating one for Dallas. The Cowboys lost again the next year in the NFC Championship Game and then slowly started a decline that led to the end of the Cowboys' first generation of greatness. Pearson said that game caused him to cry over football for the first time since high school. Jones later called it "the downfall of the Cowboys."

Between the time Clark made The Catch and the next time the Cowboys won the Super Bowl (1992), Montana, Ronnie Lott, and Clark led a crop of

49ers to four Super Bowl wins and the undisputed title of Team of the 1980s. "Freak injuries happened to our draft choices from then on," Jones told the *Dallas Morning News* in 1992. "That game gave the 49ers confidence. As for us, we had a history of when [we got a team down] it's over. We lost that. It carried over for years."

SURE, I'LL TRY THAT GAME

For a guy who didn't really want to be around, Ed "Too Tall" Jones sure stuck around a long time. Growing up in Jackson, Tennessee, "Too Tall" patrolled the hardwood and dreamed of the boxing ring. He would eventually take up his passion for the sweet science—boxing, but it was his longevity in a Cowboys uniform that would make him forever known in Dallas.

Jones didn't dominate his position, but he did revolutionize thinking about how teams could stock the defensive end spot. He didn't have a Hall of Fame career like linemate Randy White. Jones was simply a basketball player and boxer who happened upon a game he took to quickly.

He was a high school basketball starter who figured he would be heading to college on a basketball scholarship. He wanted to box, but his mother told him he needed to get a college education, especially because he was being given the opportunity to go for free. Jones decided on Tennessee State. When he got there, he tried out for the football team despite never having played in high school. During the first week of practice, Jones was hanging out in pants that didn't even cover his knees. One of his

ED JONES

Born: February 23, 1951, in Jackson, Tennessee
Nickname: "Too Tall"
Position: Defensive End
Years with the Cowboys: 1974–1978, 1980–1989
All-Pro/Pro Bowl Appearances: 2/3
Honors:

* No. 1 draft pick in 1974
* Cowboys record: 15 seasons played
* Cowboys record: 224 games played
* Member of the 1974 All-Rookie Team

teammates, noticing that he had never had a 6-foot-9 teammate before, said: "You know, you're too tall for football."

A nickname and a legend was born.

"You know, you're too tall for football."

[TENNESSEE STATE TEAMMATE]

Jones had a nice career at Tennessee State, but he really made his name once he got to the all-star circuit. Jones was invited to the 1973 Senior Bowl where he put on a show that earned him a spot on the game's all-time team. The Cowboys' scouting director Gil Brandt had seen Jones play and was convinced that he was one of the new breed of players Landry could integrate into the Flex. The Cowboys sent Billy Parks and Tody Smith down I-45 to Houston for the first pick in the draft. Dallas took "Too Tall," and he hung around Dallas until summer 1990.

WORLDLY MAN

If "Too Tall" had made a different choice, he may have had to go the boxing route. After his final college season in 1973, two leagues deemed Jones worthy of their top pick. The Cowboys took him as did the upstart World Football League.

The new league was headed by Gary L. Davidson, who had also led the renegade American Basketball Association (ABA) and World Hockey League (WHL). Jones took the Cowboys' cash instead of the opportunity with the Detroit Wheels. That opportunity would have lasted a whole 18 months. Boston, Toronto, and Washington, D.C., folded before playing a game. The Houston Texans became the Shreveport Steamers in the middle of one season. New York took off to become the Charlotte Hornets, and Detroit and Jacksonville simply folded their tents in the middle of the 1975 season. The league, which included a Honolulu team and had expansion plans for Tokyo, Madrid, and London, collapsed under heavy debt the same year.

SEASONED VET

Jones, who never missed a game, played more games than any other Cowboys player. Mark Tuinei, Bill Bates, and "Too Tall" are the only players to ever play 15 seasons in Dallas.

Jones made the all-rookie team in 1974, made three Pro Bowls, and was twice an All-Pro. His revolutionary contribution was that, because of size, he didn't always have to get to the quarterback to stop a play. He could stay put at his end spot, get his big mitts in the way, and knock the ball down. Teams started teaching the technique after Jones showed how effective it could be.

Jones came to the Cowboys in their heyday. He played in 20 playoff games, six NFC Championship games, and three Super Bowls, winning one in 1978 against Denver. Still, even on the day he retired, he admitted that football was simply something he did because he was really good at it. "Boxing has always been the No. 1 sport for me," Jones said.

Football turned out to be a convenient and profitable second choice.

CAREER CHANGE

Had his insatiable desire for contact in another area not so drawn him in, Ed "Too Tall" Jones would stand alone as the guy who played the longest with the Cowboys. "Too Tall" has always loved the fight game. He wanted to be a pro fighter when he was a kid, but momma said school first. Then, he got first-round NFL cash, which, even in 1974, was impossible to turn down in favor of boxing. So, "Too Tall" signed a four-year deal with the option for a fifth and decided he'd play through his first deal and take off.

And, that's exactly what he did. After the Cowboys beat the Broncos in the Super Bowl, Jones told Brandt and Landry he would be taking off after the next year to box. General manager Tex Schramm chalked the talk up to an interesting new way to negotiate a contract. After the 1978 Super Bowl, Jones did take off. He stepped into the ring as a 28-year-old heavyweight and accomplished a lifelong goal. "Had I not done it I would have always wondered, 'What if,'" Jones said. "It was a huge load off me that I did it. I came back in shape and was able to concentrate."

Jones went 6–0, beating tomato cans that make Peter McNeely look like Joe Louis. He even fought in front of the hometown folks, beating Jim Wallace with a second-round TKO at the Dallas Convention Center while 4,000 watched and wished for Jones to put the Cowboys' colors back on.

> **"It was a huge load off me that I did it. I came back in shape and was able to concentrate."**
>
> [ED "TOO TALL" JONES]

He returned to football the next season, but he made boxing connections that led him to try managing fighters when he retired. He became involved with Muhammad Ali, Larry Holmes, and Sugar Ray Leonard, who, along with Jones's trainer, almost talked him into returning to the squared

BELOW: Ed "Too Tall" Jones's commitment to staying in shape led to his playing and starting more games than any other Cowboys player.

circle in 1986. Jones continues to be involved in boxing-related charities and fight clubs in Dallas and Memphis. To this day he refuses to disclose why he stopped fighting. He says the boxing stint was just something he had to do. "I didn't think it would be five years [before I left]," Jones said the day he retired for good. "I think I would have retired after my third year if I hadn't signed a four-year deal with an option."

THE ORIGINAL LOW CARB-ER

"Too Tall" was low carb when low carb wasn't cool. Actually, he was low carb before anyone knew what low carb meant.

Jones never missed a game because he was always in great shape. He said his boxing training had a lot to do with his conditioning. When he was getting ready for the boxing sojourn, his daily regiment included running six miles and working the speed bag. He also adhered to a strict diet that Atkins lovers would embrace. For breakfast, Jones went with two scrambled eggs and three bacon strips. Lunch was replaced with a dinner menu of major chicken, seafood, and once-a-week red meat to fuel the "Too Tall" machine.

WINDING DOWN

Tact came later for Jerry Jones and Jimmy Johnson. When the duo arrived on the Dallas sports scene in 1989 with Jones's purchase of the Cowboys and firing of Landry, they did everything with an edge. That edge eventually led to a lot of winning. Early on, it also led to a lot of alienation.

During the regime's first season, Johnson asked "Too Tall" to move inside and try defensive tackle. "Too Tall" didn't mind the move, telling Johnson, "I want to play even if you have to put me at linebacker."

But Johnson thought it better for "Too Tall" to contribute from the bench. After a loss to Kansas City that year, Johnson publicly announced that "Too Tall" was taking a seat. That's when the Cowboys started taking a beating.

Angry calls, letters, the media, and talk shows wondered how this could be happening to a Cowboys legend. How could they just hang "Too Tall" out after he had started 198 straight games?

Johnson's team was 0–7, and he wanted to get rookie Tony Tolbert and Jim Jeffcoat more looks at end. "Too Tall" even agreed with the move, but Johnson later went back on the stance and allowed Jones's streak to continue.

Still, the writing was on the wall. A great career was coming to an end. The Cowboys were going in a different direction, and that direction included few ties to their glorious past. Jones's only sack that last season was in the Kansas City game when he corralled Steve Pelleur. It was quickly erased when Jones was called for a facemask.

After the 1989 season, Johnson traded for Danny Stubbs, one of his former Miami players, and told anyone that would listen that he really wanted Jones to retire. "When Dallas turns it around, it will be Tony Tolbert, not Ed Jones who is playing," Jones said the day Cowboys defensive coordinator Butch Davis, one year his junior, told him about being benched. "This is the move they had to make."

RANDY WHITE

The late Harvey Martin used to say Randy White was the ultimate paradox. "Off the field, he's the nicest guy in the world," Martin said, "but he gets up for games. He's just mean. That's all you can say."

White enjoyed three things during his playing days: Throwing around iron, throwing around quarterbacks, and throwing around the bull with his buddies in a fishing boat. He came to Dallas as part of the famous "Dirty Dozen" draft class of 1975. As the Cowboys' first-round pick that year, he was expected to be the leader of the 12 rookies that made that year's team. White not only led the rookies, but he also put his mark on a team that was looking for a replacement for Hall of Famer Bob Lilly.

White did fine as the fill-in, making All-Pro a team record eight times in a row, playing in nine Pro Bowls, and topping his career with a Hall of Fame induction in 1994. He played in six NFC Championship games and three Super Bowls and missed only one game in his 14-year career.

When the Cowboys were making their Super Bowl runs in the 1970s, White became the center of the new Doomsday Defense. Charlie Waters, a defensive back on those teams, said he has still yet to see anyone that dominated up front like White did. He was the rare combination of speed, size, strength, intelligence, and just plain intensity. White said he "lived for Sundays. Just that emotion you get right before you go out. Every emotion is running through your body. There's nothing quite like it."

One day during their playing days, Waters was asked to describe his

RANDY WHITE

Born: January 15, 1953, in Pittsburgh, Pennsylvania
Nickname: "The Manster"
Position: Defensive Tackle
Years with the Cowboys: 1975–1988
All-Pro/Pro Bowl Appearances: 8/9
Honors:
∗ Cowboys record: 8 All-Pro selections
∗ Cowboys: 2nd career solo tackles (701)
∗ Cowboys: 3rd career combined tackles (1,104)
∗ Cowboys: 3rd games played (209)
∗ Super Bowl XII Co-MVP
∗ Defensive Player of the Year in 1978
∗ NFL Defensive Lineman of the Year in 1982
∗ Inducted into the Ring of Honor in 1994
∗ Inducted into the Pro Football Hall of Fame in 1994

defensive teammate. "Randy White," Waters said, "is 'The Manster.' He's half man, half monster."

The nickname stuck, but it was one three years in the making. When White was drafted, coach Tom Landry didn't think he was going to be big enough to play his college position. The year before, the Cowboys had taken 6-foot-9 Ed "Too Tall" Jones to anchor one defensive end spot. Two years prior, Harvey Martin and his 6-foot-5, 262-pound frame hit town. The two defensive ends reflected the direction of the team. Landry wanted to get quicker and use athletes such as Martin and Jones in positions and in ways the league had yet to see. To Landry, it was all about exploiting matchups. That's why he thought White, no small guy at 6-foot-4 and 257 pounds, would make a good middle linebacker.

Lee Roy Jordan was on the backside of his career when White arrived. Landry drafted White with the thought that he would be the next great Cowboys linebacker. When he arrived in Dallas, "The Manster" traded his college number 94 for No. 54 because he was told he was making the switch. The first year (1975) was tough on White, although it was offset by the team's surprising run to the Super Bowl in a season that included Drew Pearson's famous "Hail Mary" catch against Minnesota in the playoffs. White played in all 14 games, but he made only 19 tackles, seven of which were sacks.

The next year, he upped the total to 42 stops with six sacks, but he still wasn't comfortable with the position or his surroundings. "When I got to Dallas out of Maryland, everything intimidated me," he said. "The city, the team, my position. It was all intimidating."

Defensive coordinator Ernie Stautner, a Hall of Fame defensive lineman, took White in. He was extremely tough on his pupil but took a keen interest during the 1976 season because he thought something was bothering the young man. White told Stautner, who is still one of his main men, that the linebacker position just didn't feel right to him. He said he got comfortable playing tackle in college and wouldn't mind another shot at the spot. Stautner and Landry discussed the situation and decided to let White give it a go for the first time in 1977.

The response was a 118-tackle and 13-sack year and the first of the eight straight All-Pro seasons. The Cowboys went 15–2, sparked thoughts of "best team ever?" with only five wins by seven or fewer points, and crushed Denver 27–10 in the Super Bowl. In that game, in front of a then-record 102 million television viewers, White was being "The Manster." He lived alongside Broncos quarterback Craig Morton. He hurried, harassed, and haggled the former Cowboy into four interceptions, the same number Morton completed to his own guys. Denver ended with only eight completions and 35 net passing yards. White's day wasn't finished. He was also part of a unit that forced four fumbles and held the Broncos to 156 total yards. White shared co-MVP honors that day with Harvey Martin, joining former Cowboy Chuck Howley and Miami's Victor Scott as the only defensive players, at that time, to ever win a Super Bowl MVP. "That year everything was finally right," White said. "I didn't feel comfortable those first couple of years. What I really remember is Lee Roy Jordan taking me under his wing and really helping me out. He was a great leader and really helped me ease into a lot of things."

The next season was White's best, racking up 123 tackles and 16 sacks on his way to winning NFC Defensive Player of the Year honors. Back at tackle and finally comfortable, "The Manster" had arrived.

BRINGING A LOAD

Had White stayed his original course, he might have been scoring touchdowns instead of preventing them. When White first arrived at Maryland, the Terrapins were not a good program. White had chosen the school because it was close to his hometown of Wilmington, Delaware, and he wanted his family to see him play. The Terps hadn't had a winning season since 1962, but they figured the local kid would help them turn that around. Jerry Claiborne took over for Ray Lester before the 1971 season, and things did slowly start to turn around. Maryland went 5–5–1 that season, not a winning year, but one that got the ship righted.

That season, Claiborne noticed his strongest and one of his quickest players was his fullback. Needing to shore up the defensive front and wanting his best athletes on defense, Claiborne asked the fullback if he wouldn't mind moving across the line. White said he would give it a shot.

At first, size was a concern. Offensive linemen were slowly starting to creep up to the high 200s in weight, and defensive linemen were trying to keep pace. Claiborne's philosophy, however, was that if no one could lay a hand on his defensive linemen, they couldn't be blocked. White was already quick, and he developed soft hands and smooth feet while in the offensive backfield. He had natural speed and actually got faster as his college career progressed. Claiborne figured White could dominate the interior because, although he was only 248 pounds at the time, White was already stronger than most ACC offensive linemen.

> **"He was quicker than anyone he played against, almost always stronger and his intensity was unmatched."**
> [JERRY CLAIBORNE]

During the two years White played up front, Maryland went 16–8 and went to a bowl game for the first time in 18 years. White developed a passion for the weight room and dominated offenses in his last season when he had 12 sacks. "He was simply unstoppable," the late Claiborne used to say of White. "He was quicker than anyone he played against, almost always stronger and his intensity was unmatched."

THAT SUMS IT UP

White had news, and he needed to let someone know about it. The Maryland defensive lineman had absolutely dominated college football in 1974, and he was starting to get recognized. He had already been named the ACC Player of the Year and a consensus All-America choice was about to come his way. When the big-time awards started to be handed out, the ox-strong White got plenty of calls. He just didn't make very many.

Although he was never soft-spoken and became much chattier after his playing days, White the player simply said what he felt and he got to the point.

After leading Maryland to a conference title in 1974, White won the Lombardi Award and the Outland Trophy. While sitting around he got a call from his father, Guy. The World War II veteran was thrilled for his son and had put in a call of congrats.

"Oh, you heard," Randy asked.

"Yeah," replied the former army paratrooper.

"Okay," college football's best defensive player said, "good night."

DIRTY DOZEN

The Cowboys were in need of a spark. The team was coming off a 1974 season that, though it kept the consecutive winning seasons streak alive, was not a Cowboys-like year. The team started 1–4, finished with wins in seven of the last nine, but it just seemed nothing lined up right.

The previous year, plans were announced for a new league. The World Football League was going to directly take on the established league and that started with taking some of their players. During the 1974 season, the WFL began getting commitments from several name players. Calvin Hill, D.D. Lewis, and Pat Toomay had all signed WFL contracts and would be taking off at season's end. Quarterback Roger Staubach had his worst year as a starter, completing less than 53 percent of his passes and throwing more interceptions (15) than touchdowns (11), the only time either happened in his career. Although about to set the team record for receptions in a year, Drew Pearson suffered a knee injury in the final game against the Raiders and fell three grabs shy. It was an anomaly season, the first time the team had missed the playoffs since 1965 and the only time the postseason went Cowboys-less from 1966 to 1984.

General manager Tex Schramm felt the team was aging. He needed to get impact players to replace some established veterans, especially on defense. Going into the 1975 draft, Dallas had the second pick via a trade with the New York Giants and their original No. 18 pick. After Atlanta took California quarterback Steve Bartkowski, the Cowboys, feeling they needed an impact defender, grabbed White, leaving the Chicago Bears to take Walter Payton two picks later.

With the 18th choice, Dallas went "Hollywood" with Langston linebacker Thomas Henderson. Then came guard Burton Lawless in the second round. Arizona State linebacker Bob Breunig, one of White's and Henderson's Doomsday buddies, was up next followed by Pat Donovan of Stanford, who was a defensive end in college but ended up playing nine years at offensive tackle in Dallas. Oklahoma teammates Kyle Davis and Randy Hughes made the squad. "Too Tall" Jones's Tennessee State teammate Mike Hegman joined the group in the seventh round and hung around 12 years. In the 13th round, the Cowboys picked up guard Herb Scott, a 10-year Cowboy.

In total, 12 rookies made the roster and helped what many thought would be a rebuilding year for the Cowboys to turn into the team's third Super Bowl appearance. The draft is still the most productive haul in Cowboys history.

FAMILY AFFAIR

White used to love playing on the East Coast. He loved beating the Redskins, taking it to the Eagles, and watching New Yorkers moan when the Giants lost. Any return to the East Coast also meant his family from nearby Delaware would be able to attend the game. One Monday night in the nation's capital, White wished his family had stayed home.

Despite playing in heated enemy territory, White's mother, Laverne, always wore her Cowboys gear. That night, the game got close, the yelling got louder, and the actions eventually got out of hand. A Washington fan found out the two women sitting beside him cheering for Dallas were Randy White's mom and sister. After an exchange, the man poured beer on the sister's head, not knowing that another White was sitting a row behind. White's brother came over the seats and punched the fan. Before the beer had settled, White's mom also got into the act, knocking the man around a bit before they were separated. "Mom was a Cowboys fan," White said.

CROSSING THE LINE

When negotiating his final contract, White tried to set himself and his family on the financial freedom trail. As part of the deal, White got a $6 million annuity that would pay him an equal amount for up to 20 years after he retired. White would receive his money if the Cowboys cut him or if he suffered a career-ending injury. The loophole was that if he failed to render services anytime during his contract, the team could suspend his payments or have the option to get out of the agreement entirely.

That didn't seem to be a problem for a player who had missed one game since he stepped into a Cowboys uniform in 1975. The fine print, which eventually led to what White called one of the lowlights of his career, was that if the player could not fulfill his club obligation for whatever reasons other than "an act of God rendering player performance physically impossible," the team didn't have to live up to their financial end of the bargain.

Although players association head Gene Upshaw may have considered it one, the 1987 NFL players' strike didn't qualify as "an act of God." Two games into that year, players walked out on the owners, who lost one week before using replacement players for three weeks. One position the Cowboys didn't have to replace was defensive tackle.

White was in the twilight of his career and would only play the 1987 and 1988 season before retiring. A neck injury had started to bother him, affecting both his play and his desire to be financially set the rest of his life. White and Don Smereck talked about how they would vote on the eve of the decision to strike. White told Smereck he was going to vote "no strike" because he couldn't afford to jeopardize the annuity payments that would kick in when he retired. Smereck said he understood and would join his buddy as a picket line crosser.

The decision was not well received. Linebacker Jeff Rohrer and tight end Doug Cosbie, who was the Cowboys' player representative, shouted at White the first day he pulled his Ford truck into the player parking lot. Rohrer, who would return about a month later and play behind White, called the future Hall of Famer "a scab for life."

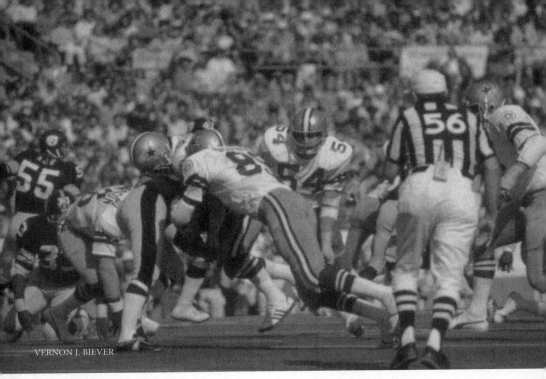

VERNON J. BIEVER

ABOVE: Randy White (54) was simply a football player, making All-Pro a team-record eight times.

Running back Tony Dorsett, who went into the Ring of Honor and Hall of Fame with White on the same day, told *The Dallas Morning News* that "as a team captain, he let the team down. But, he's going to make the All-Pro list this year—the 'Scabs' All-Pro list."

Dorsett finished his comments by branding White "Captain Scab."

Not long after, Dorsett found out that the annuity he had in his contract had the same stipulations White's did. Sit out and you might lose your nest egg.

A week after calling White names, it was picket-breaker Dorsett scoring touchdowns for the Cowboys' replacements in front of the 40,000 that showed up at Texas Stadium to watch the Cowboys mixed bag take on Philadelphia's gaggle of spares. "I knew [there would be resentment] when I crossed," White said on the day he crossed, while sitting in his normal locker, between two stranger teammates, Javan Ross and Rayotis Brown. "I don't have anything against what they're doing, but I had to do what was best for me. There's really not a whole lot else to say about it."

RING "MANSTER"

Randy White has always been an original. Strolls around his locker would turn up fishing gear, cow patty candles, maybe some steer roping gear. He was an East Coast guy that went to the University of Maryland, but his accent and his love for the country life is almost Walt Garrison-like natural. He owns a ranch not far from former Cowboy Deion Sanders, used to train dogs, prefers a ribeye to red wine, and, while looking for yet another edge, turned to the martial arts in the middle of his career. He appeared in Long John Silvers commercials with his mother and in beer ads with former New York Jets lineman Joe Klecko. White wore No. 54 while playing on the interior line. He crossed the picket line during a strike, causing major internal strife that led him to be branded anything but the Hall of Famer he is. He went into both the Ring of Honor and Hall of Fame with Tony Dorsett, a man who called him a lot of those names. He's been a restaurant owner, a pitchman for Internet gambling services, and even a boxer. Not a boxer like a "Too Tall" Jones boxer, but a Toughman-like boxer. Actually, exactly like a Toughman boxer.

In late 2001, a promoter with FOX's *Toughman* show offered White a chance to box Klecko on TV for three one-minute rounds. White initially turned down the chance. But he made the mistake of mentioning the offer to friends. Eventually, he got talked into taking the fight on a dare. White didn't need the money, but he needed the challenge. He rehabbed his numerous injuries and got in great shape. In January 2002, he flew to Las Vegas and beat up his buddy, knocking Klecko out in the second round. It was vintage White. Perhaps out of place, definitely out of the ordinary. It was just "The Manster" being "The Manster."

RIGHT: Against a friend or against a legend, "The Manster" wanted to win.

TONY DORSETT

Tony Dorsett was just supposed to give the Cowboys breathing room. It was a meaningless game in a somewhat meaningless year. The 1982 strike had cancelled eight games early in the season, but the NFL resumed in late November like nothing had happened other than an extended vacation. At 6–3, Dallas had the playoffs' second overall position secured. The Cowboys would get a game the next week at Texas Stadium whether or not they showed up in Minneapolis that Monday night in early January. A Vikings' win and Dallas would run with Tamp Bay. A victory Dallas' way, and it was these same two teams the next week at the other end of the country.

Despite leading the NFC in rushing for the only time in his career, Dorsett wasn't having a Dorsett-like year production-wise. His 4.1-yard average was the worst he had put up in his six years in the league. The average got quite a boost early in the fourth quarter on a play that any Cowboys fan of that era remembers, and one that can only be duplicated, but never surpassed.

Ten seconds into the fourth quarter, Cowboys quarterback Danny White threw a pass that defensive end Mark Mullaney tipped right to the waiting arms of John Turner. Turner scampered 33 yards to give the Vikings a 24–13 lead. The interception must have had a deep effect on Timmy Newsome. On the ensuing kickoff, Newsome fielded the ball in the end zone but fumbled out of bounds at the one-yard line. Now, an offense with a quarterback that had just thrown an interception for a touchdown two plays earlier was back on the field. Needing room to operate, Cowboys coach Tom Landry called for White to hand the ball off to Dorsett and let him work his magic.

Evidently, the Turner interception must have had a profound impact on Dorsett's fullback, Ron Springs, as well. When the offense trotted on to the field, Springs was nowhere to be found. No one said anything in the huddle. No one said anything after the Cowboys lined up. White didn't call time. It was like a collective haze was hovering over that side of the Metrodome.

White snapped the ball and handed to Dorsett. With no Springs, he didn't get a lead block. Dorsett hit the hole hard and was suddenly 20 yards downfield. Cornerback Willie Teal had an angle and caught Dorsett around the Dallas 30-yard line. Instead of delivering a normal Dorsett juke, he swatted Teal aside and kept going. He crossed midfield, and folks started sensing something big was happening. He didn't have Bob Hayes-like speed, but Dorsett wasn't getting caught. He ambled across the goal line and had NFL history. He had just run goal line to goal line, a 99-yard touchdown run with only 10 guys on his side.

The run beat the old NFL record by two yards and surpassed a mark that had stood since 1949. It also broke the Cowboys' team record for the longest run from scrimmage, something Dorsett already had with his 84-yard touchdown run against Philadelphia his rookie year.

"I'm in awe of that play and that man."

[BUD GRANT]

The historic jaunt is one of *Monday Night Football*'s greatest moments. However, the game didn't end up being memorable for Dallas or for Dorsett. Springs eventually found his way back into the game to give Dallas a 27–24 lead with just over six minutes left. Then, Minnesota's Tommy Kramer led a late drive that ended when he hit Rickey Young at the Cowboys' eight. Young made a sliding catch and then got treated like he had an incurable disease. The Vikings wideout was lying on the Metrodome turf, no Dallas defender slid over to lay a finger on him. So Young got up, walked into the end zone with 1:52 left and gave Minnesota a 31–27 win.

That the Cowboys lost was no big thing for Dorsett. The team was in the playoffs, and he had just put his name forever in the record book. But it's a good thing he's got tape of the play, because that's

TONY DORSETT

Born: April 7, 1954, in Rochester, Pennsylvania
Position: Running Back
Years with the Cowboys: 1977–1987
All-Pro/Pro Bowl Appearances: 1/4
Honors:
* NFL record: 99-yard touchdown run in 1983
* NFL: 4th all-time career rushing (12,036)
* Cowboys record: 1,007 all-time rookie rushing yards gained
* Cowboys: 2nd all-time career touchdowns (86)
* Cowboys: 2nd all-time career rushing yards gained (12,036)
* Named Rookie of the Year in 1977
* Heisman Trophy in 1976
* Inducted into the Ring of Honor in 1994
* Inducted into the Pro Football Hall of Fame in 1994

all he has. After scoring, an exhausted Dorsett spiked the ball and then started celebrating with his teammates. The referee grabbed the ball and tossed it to the side, and Dorsett never saw it again.

Not long after, letters started pouring Dorsett's way from people informing him that somehow they had suddenly become NFL or Vikings officials and had gotten their hands on the ball. For a nominal fee, these new league employees would be happy to let Tony D have it back. Dorsett never paid anyone for the ball, because he said he knew exactly where the ball went. "[The Vikings] were tossing it around the next day in practice," Dorsett said.

Dorsett said he is frequently asked about the run even though he doesn't think it was the best carry of his career. Which one was the best? Well, there are options. Of the top seven longest runs in Cowboys history, Dorsett has five of them, two of which came his rookie year. He also has the team's second-longest pass reception, hauling in a 91-yarder from Roger Staubach in 1978.

But those plays are mere side notes to a run that, although it came in a side note game, will forever keeps Dorsett's name in NFL lights. "It was just a fortunate time and a fortunate play for me" is how Dorsett routinely describes it. After the game, Minnesota coach Bud Grant went a little further: "I'm in awe of that play and that man."

HEADLINING

Alquippa, Pennsylvania, is only 30 miles from the University of Pittsburgh. For Dorsett, it might as well have been 3,000 miles away. Dorsett arrived on campus in the fall of 1973. He was a 155-pound freshman expected to lead a Panthers team that had had little success. Johnny Majors had moved over from Iowa State, and the freshman was going to be his go-to guy.

In his first game, Dorsett ran for 100 yards as Pittsburgh fought to a surprising 7–7 tie at powerful Georgia. Two months later, eventual champion Notre Dame popped the Panthers but did so while watching Dorsett run through their defense for 209 yards.

Dorsett went more than 1,000 yards for the season and led the team to its first bowl game in 17 years.

The 1,000-yard season was the first of four straight; he was the first college player to reach the treasured mark in four consecutive campaigns.

After that first year, though, Dorsett wanted to go home. He felt alone, wasn't enjoying himself despite the accolades, and was ready to give it up. His mother begged him to stay, calling coaches to see if there was anything they could do. Then-assistant coach Jackie Sherrill sat down with Dorsett that summer. He reminded him of his teammates who saw him as a leader and a friend. Sherrill also told him that if he stuck around a while, he might just have a nice payday waiting three years down the road.

In 1975, Dorsett, now up to 192 pounds, again shredded the Irish. He piled up 303 yards, only this time Pittsburgh won, the school's first win over Notre Dame since 1963.

The next year, Dorsett capped his senior season by running for 1,948 yards and winning the Heisman by one of the largest margins ever. Against Penn State, he ran for 224 and two touchdowns to help Pittsburgh run the table and earn a Sugar Bowl date with Georgia, the team Dorsett started his career against. He ran up 202 yards on the Louisiana Superdome turf, the same place Dallas would win the Super Bowl the next year, as Pittsburgh dismantled the Bulldogs 24–3 for the national title.

With Dorsett done, Majors high tailed it back to Tennessee. The school retired Dorsett's jersey, and he left with an NCAA-record 6,082 rushing yards, a mark that has since been passed by Wisconsin's Ron Dayne and Texas' Ricky Williams.

Good thing the skinny freshman decided to stick around.

THE FIRST BIG TRADE

Dorsett had seen a Heisman Trophy running back get exiled to a faraway place with a faraway-from-contending team. In 1968, USC running back O.J. Simpson wrapped up the Heisman and then packed a U-Haul for a cross-country banishment to Buffalo.

In no way did Dorsett want to be Act II.

In the 1977 draft, Seattle, only two years removed from expansion, had the second pick. Although Dorsett had won the Heisman, Tampa Bay, with former USC coach John McKay now guiding their fortunes, had already committed to taking his former Trojan running back Ricky Bell. The Seahawks wanted Dorsett, but he wanted no part of the Pacific Northwest. He said he would take his game to Canada before he would to Washington state. That's when Gil Brandt and Tex Schramm started working their magic.

When Brandt was hired, he brought along a sophisticated way of scouting players. He was genius at finding small college and free agents, but he also did detailed analysis of the top players. In short, Brandt was the best in the business at knowing who could play and who couldn't.

"Our running game had been weak for about three years. It was really nice to see Tony come along."

[ROGER STAUBACH]

Before coming to the Cowboys, Schramm previously worked at CBS Sports. While prepping for the 1960 Winter Olympics in Squaw Valley, he met folks affiliated with International Business Machines, better known today as IBM. Not long after taking over the Cowboys, Schramm consulted with his IBM buddies to see if there was any way they might be able to help Schramm's team get better. The company developed a very high-level scouting program that didn't necessarily tell the team who was destined for greatness. But it did tell who was likely headed for the spare file. In this draft, the computer said, "Beware of Ricky Bell."

That in mind, Schramm went into full Schramm mode. He played the "Dorsett to Canada" card like it was the missing ace in a royal flush. Like most high-stakes battles, Schramm won. Seattle backed down, giving in to Schramm's offer of the Cowboys' first-round pick and three second-rounders. Dallas got Dorsett. Seattle got Steve August, Tom Lynch, Terry Beeson, and Pete Cronan.

Not long after making the deal, Brandt made a congratulatory call to Schramm. "Book rooms for the Super Bowl," Brandt told his boss.

Dorsett was the Rookie of the Year and had a 1,000-yard season. The Cowboys thrashed Denver 27–10 in the year's Super Bowl, with Dorsett running for 66 yards and a touchdown.

CARRYING THE LOAD

Had Seattle called Schramm's bluff in the 1977 draft, the Cowboys would have been in trouble. Roger Staubach was leading the Cowboys to Super Bowls, but he was doing so without much tailback help. Calvin Hill had back-to-back 1,000-yard seasons in 1972 and 1973, the only two times a Cowboys back had reached the mark in team history. After the 1974 season, Hill took off for the World Football League and Dallas took off on a three-year wild goose chase for

BELOW: Tony Dorsett tries to eek out extra yardage against the Steelers in Super Bowl XIII.

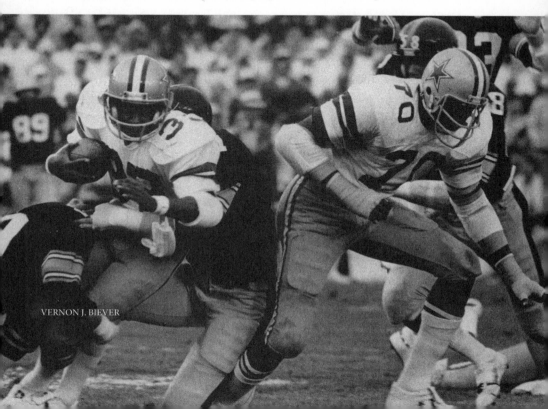

VERNON J. BIEVER

a running back. Fullback Robert Newhouse led the team in rushing in 1975. Doug Dennison had the highlight of his five-year career in 1976, topping the Cowboys' rushing charts with a massive 542-yard effort. "Our running game had been weak for about three years," Staubach said. "It was really nice to see Tony come along."

Dorsett introduced himself to the town by rushing for 1,007 yards, his first of five straight 1,000-yard seasons (eight straight taking away the strike-shortened 1982 season). His 1977 arrival came at the ideal time. Dallas was still a veteran enough team that the Cowboys only needed to replace parts rather than the whole to make Super Bowl runs. That gave Dorsett time to adjust to life in Dallas and to the pro game.

He didn't need much time adjusting to the game. Socially, he did. Sherrill's prediction was right. The big dough came in the form a $1.1 million contract. Big Time Dorsett hit Dallas and immediately got into a bar fight. He bought a phat Lincoln Continental and engraved his initials over each door handle. He also told reporters that his name was French. Pronounce it Dor-SETT he demanded.

This didn't sit well with the mostly conservative Dallas fan base that wanted their manchild to just run the ball, win games, and shut his mouth. The first impression started a career-long love-hate relationship with Cowboys fans. The attitude also didn't sit well with coach Tom Landry.

Landry benched Dorsett for most of the Philadelphia game at Texas Stadium in his rookie season because Dorsett failed to call to explain his absence from an early-morning walk-through. Dorsett had family in from Pennsylvania, but Landry didn't care. He thought Dorsett had a lackadaisical attitude toward the game, and it needed to change. Dorsett didn't see the down-the-road view that Landry had, calling his coach "unfair." Even Cowboys fans didn't appreciate the rookie challenging the legend, booing Dorsett for the first time in a loss to Minnesota the next week.

Landry was patient, though, because he knew that Staubach was about to retire. The Cowboys would have to turn their fortunes over to Danny White, and he needed a rock-solid leader. He needed Dorsett to be that guy.

After Staubach left in 1979, Landry sat Dorsett down and told him what the team needed and what Dorsett needed to do to help. Dorsett listened, showing that he might be maturing somewhat. He also experienced personal loss that year when his fiancée died of a rare nerve disorder.

Perhaps looking for an escape, Dorsett got in the weight room, trying to make himself, at Landry's behest, a more durable back. He rushed for 1,185 yards in 1980. The next season, the one that ended with Dwight Clark's catch, was Dorsett's best. He was named team captain and ran for a then-Cowboys record 1,646 yards, averaging a career-tying best 4.8 yards-per-tote.

He still battled fans, Landry, and personal demons, but he had finally become the Cowboys' offensive leader.

LESSONS LEARNED

June 1984 to August 1985 were not good times for Dorsett. Lessons came, as they often do, in the cruelest of ways. His wife filed for divorce in June, and then his father died during the 1984 season. While preparing for the 1985 season, he got a phone call from Uncle Sam letting him know that the government wasn't really concerned that he was headed toward 10,000 yards that year. They needed the $414,000 he owed in back taxes. He then found out he wouldn't be able to use the money from an oil deal his agent arranged because that $600,000 had been lost. A bank had to file a lawsuit to get payment on a loan worth more than $150,000.

Dorsett went to the organization and asked for help. The team helped him settle his divorce and then lent him $240,000 to make the tax man go away. To show his appreciation, Dorsett failed to report to camp, holding out until mid-August and demanding an extension. The Cowboys relented again, giving Dorsett two more years, giving him $750,000 worth of real estate and adding the annuity that would eventually make him taste his words. "The Cowboys were a really big part of Tony Dorsett," coach Tom Landry told the *Dallas Morning News* not long after he was fired in 1989, a year after Dorsett bolted for Denver. "They came in and helped him [financially] when he needed help, and he never could return that kind of favor. I would have liked for him to stay here, but he didn't want to. That was disappointing."

The old saying goes that it's best not to step on people on your way up the ladder because they are the same people you'll meet on your way down.

> "They came in and helped him [financially] when he needed help and he never could return that kind of favor. I would have liked for him to stay here, but he didn't want to. That was disappointing."
>
> [TOM LANDRY]

Dorsett learned that the hard way during the 1987 players' strike. It was a hardline strike. Players were prepared to sit as long as they thought they needed to for owners to cave. Thing is, some people forgot previous agreements.

In the summer of 1985, Dorsett had run into financial trouble. The team bailed him out and then extended his contract through 1989. As part of the extension, Dorsett received a $6 million annuity, much like Randy White and Danny White had gotten. Just like the Whites, Dorsett had wording in his deal that required him to perform or risk losing money.

The first week the league used replacement players, Dorsett sat out, joining the picket lines and labeling Randy White "Captain Scab" for crossing the picket line. The team had already let Dorsett know he was risking his annuity by not playing. When Dorsett found out he stood to lose as much as $3 million from the annuity that was likely going to set him up for his financial future, all of the sudden that hard line union stance wasn't as appealing.

Dorsett was back in uniform the next week against Philadelphia. When he scored on a 10-yard run, fans, upset at his comments and that he demanded a contract extension before the season started, booed the future Hall of Famer.

THE DREAM BACKFIELD

It was the dream situation. Two Heisman Trophy-winning backs in one backfield. One a slashing, find-the-hole veteran. The other a brickhouse-built machine that could catch passes and float around defenders as easily as he could plow over them.

Herschel Walker and Tony Dorsett: two of the greatest college runners ever in the same backfield on "America's Team." It was supposed to be a dream. It turned out to be the nightmare that led to Dorsett's departure.

In 1985, Dallas spent a fifth-round pick on Walker and prayed failure on a competitor. The Georgia running back had signed a massive contract with the USFL's New Jersey Generals three years earlier and had few Cowboys plans. He probably didn't think the USFL would be bankrupt after three years, that he would end up with assets valued at exactly three dollars not long after, and that he would be looking for a gig.

Walker signed a five-year deal with Dallas and hit town in 1986. He was greeted with a Dorsett tirade. Dorsett was upset that Walker had a $1 million salary compared to his $450,000. Dorsett threatened to go AWOL, obviously forgetting the financial trouble the team bailed him out of not even a year earlier.

The two tried to coexist, but it never worked. Dorsett led the team in rushing in 1986 but had only 748 yards on 184 carries, the fewest ever in his nine full seasons. Landry was trying to mix and match the two depending on the situation. Walker was used mostly as a fullback and pass catcher; Dorsett still the tailback. Landry was trying to exploit the duo's very different talents. Dorsett saw it another way. He thought the team was disrespecting him and his talent.

Dorsett lost three games to a knee injury in 1986, snapping a 94-consecutive-starts streak. Then came the strike-shortened 1987 season. He needed just over 700 yards to pass Jim Brown for second place on the NFL's all-time rushing list. He got only 456 and didn't lead the team in rushing for the first time in 10 years. In a game against New England, Walker got 28 chances, going for 173 yards. The Patriots saw Dorsett one time.

He exploded after the game, questioning why Cowboys coaches couldn't get both guys on the field at the same time. Dorsett said he wanted out.

There were no takers until early June of the next year when Dorsett's old running backs coach, Dan Reeves, then the Broncos head coach, said he wouldn't mind Tony D in Denver.

DENVER DISASTER

Dorsett can give Emmitt Smith a lot of advice. Records are nice, but it's better to protect your legacy. Dorsett in a Broncos uniform was equal to O.J.'s 49ers years, Willie Mays with the Mets, or maybe Emmitt Smith with the Cardinals.

On the day he left the Cowboys he proclaimed that "Tony Dorsett will be beginning a new chapter in his career."

The chapter lasted about 18 months. Dorsett got his chances in the Rockies. He carried 181 times in 1988 for 703 yards. He passed Jim Brown for second place on the all-time rushing list, but he averaged only 3.9 yards-per-carry, the second worst of his career. The next year, Dorsett suffered a knee injury during training camp and called it quits.

Now 64, Dorsett spends his time with a number of area businesses. Despite his issues, he looks back on his Dallas days fondly. He understands there were mistakes made, but he believes his good times (a Super Bowl ring and four Pro Bowl selections) will always shine through both for him and the fans. He was inducted into the Cowboys' Ring of Honor alongside Randy White in 1994, the same year both went into the Hall of Fame. "When you're playing you feel like you're giving so much to a franchise," Dorsett said upon his Ring induction. "For the franchise to recognize you for what you've been able to bring is quite rewarding."

KEVIN LEVINE/GETTY IMAGES

MICHAEL IRVIN

To this day, it is get in, fasten your seat belt, and let's go with Michael Irvin. No. 88's focus is a little different now, but when "The Playmaker" was making plays for the Cowboys, there was no one who went harder on the field, and no one who even came close to how hard he went off it.

Irvin was "Hollywood" Henderson with major talent and major desire. There has never been a fiercer competitor to come through Dallas. It didn't matter if it was a defender trying to stop him or someone trying to out-party him. Irvin wanted to win.

Man, did Irvin ever have a good time. For any Cowboys fan, Irvin was everything you wanted on the field. You knew every Monday morning your paper wouldn't have a better receiving performance on Sunday. Because of Irvin, the Cowboys won three Super Bowls in a four-year span and fans got to see one of this generation's greatest receivers and showmen.

Even before he got to the Cowboys, Irvin's competitive fire was well known. Not long after signing his Miami scholarship, Irvin, still in high school, showed up in Coral Gables. While leaning against a goalpost

MICHAEL IRVIN

Born: March 5, 1966, in Fort Lauderdale, Florida
Nickname: "The Playmaker"
Position: Wide Receiver
Years with Cowboys: 1988–1999
All-Pro/Pro Bowl Appearances: 3/5
Honors:
* NFL record: 11 100-yard receiving games in a single season (1995)
* NFL record: 7 consecutive 100-yard receiving games in a single season (1995)
* Cowboys record: 750 career receptions
* Cowboys record: 11,904 career receiving yards
* Cowboys record: 87 career playoff receptions
* Cowboys record: 1,315 career playoff yards
* Cowboys record: 8 playoff receiving touchdowns (tied)
* Cowboys record: 111 receptions in a single season (1995)
* Cowboys record: 1,603 yards in a single season (1995)
* Holds Cowboys' top five single-season yardage marks
* Holds Cowboys' top three single-season receptions marks
* Seven 1,000-yard seasons
* 47 100-yard receiving games
* Inducted into the Pro Football Hall of Fame in 2007
* Inducted into the Ring of Honor in 2005

wearing shades and big gold, Irvin announced to anyone listening that he would have the receiver job soon.

As a Hurricane, he fought, pushed off, and ran around his own defensive backs like he was playing a New Year's Day game. Former assistant Butch Davis told the *Dallas Morning News* before the 2004 draft that Miami was able to produce so much professional talent because of the practice precedent players such as Irvin set. "You can't imagine what Bennie Blades and Irvin did to one another in practice," Davis said. "They went after each other like they were playing for the national championship every day."

"Whether it's playing dominoes. Or basketball. Or practicing," said then-Cowboys coach Dave Campo on the day Irvin retired, "Michael has that little something extra that makes it important for him to be the best."

Although his college coach, Jimmy Johnson, was named Cowboys coach in 1989, it was actually Tom Landry who drafted "The Playmaker" in 1988. Irvin suffered an ACL injury in October of his rookie season but was back a year later to get to work in earnest on the Cowboys' record book.

In a 12-year career that spanned four of the Cowboys' six coaches, Irvin led the team in receiving a team-record eight straight times. When Irvin broke the Cowboys' record for receptions in a season with 93 in 1991, he did so by 17 catches. Before he was done, Irvin had the top three receptions seasons in team history and the top *five* yardage marks. From 1991 to 1995, Irvin's average year was 90 catches, 1,419 yards, and seven touchdowns. He finished his career as the Cowboys' leading receiver by almost 4,000 yards ahead of Drew Pearson.

No one ran crisper routes or worked more in tune in the early 1990s with quarterback Troy Aikman in Dallas's timing offense than the man with "The Playmaker" license plate on his Mercedes. Never a huge touchdown producer, Irvin was the receiver defensive backs actually feared seeing come over the middle. The Cowboys won Super Bowl titles with the Aikman-to-Irvin slant setting up Alvin Harper's gamebreakers and Emmitt Smith's consistent "pound at you until you break" routine.

The Triplets attack of Aikman, Smith, and Irvin were, in order, the head, heart, and soul of those great teams. Aikman was the precise perfectionist. Smith was the warrior. Irvin was the fiery leader who would light up a lazy teammate as quickly as he would a cheating corner. Fans debated which one was more important, but each of the three knew that without one of the parts the whole body died.

Irvin was the first to go, succumbing to a neck injury and retiring in the summer of 2000. The body went when Aikman followed Irvin into retirement a year later because of concussions. Emmitt Smith took off for Arizona after the 2002 season, and the monster was dead. The Triplets era was over; the legend was just beginning.

WORKHORSE

During the 1990s, opposing fans disdained Irvin for the exact reason Cowboys fans loved him. He simply made plays when plays needed to be made. Irvin wasn't a game-breaking wideout. He preferred a 10-yard in route to a highlight-grabbing fly pattern. He enjoyed going over the middle to make the in-traffic receptions receivers still fear. If it was third and seven, Irvin preferred getting eight yards and getting up to signal first down to blowing by a corner down the sideline for six points. Among the team's top 10 longest passes, Irvin was involved in only one of them, an 87-yarder from Aikman against Phoenix in 1992.

Irvin had his share of scores, but he set up even more. Smith is the all-time leading rusher in NFL history because of some of the greatest offensive lines in history. A lot of praise also goes to his buddy on the outside. With tight end Jay Novacek and Irvin, the Cowboys of the 1990s had one of the best clutch receiving duos in league history. Rarely could a team blitz Dallas because Aikman often saw it coming, audibled for Irvin to run a quick slant route, and then hit "The Playmaker" with flawless execution. When teams began blitzing cornerbacks instead of stunting linebackers, Irvin would break off his slant route and either go upfield and battle a safety for the ball or go straight up the field and battle often shorter and weaker corners for a pass. Opponents complained Irvin pushed off. Irvin maintained he was simply a master of position.

Either way, Irvin took one vital defensive aspect completely out of opponents' repertoires. Not being able to blitz the Cowboys meant a lot of straight, man-on-man blocking, where the 1990s Cowboys were simply superior. It meant a lot of yards for Smith, a lot of time for Aikman, and a lot of man-on-man coverage for speed demon Alvin Harper.

Irvin is third in team history in receiving touchdowns, but that was not his specialty. He was the workhorse receiver both in games and in practice. He averaged almost 16.0 yards a catch for his career. He made his living by being the soul of the team, relishing the plays and situations other receivers shunned.

Much of that desire and success came because Irvin was so well prepared. Former Cowboys defensive coordinator Butch Davis coached Irvin both at the University of Miami and in Dallas. He said he never saw anyone practice as intensely as Irvin. That dedication is why Irvin and Aikman ended up being such good friends. Wanting everything and everyone around him to be perfect, Aikman had nothing to worry about on the outside. Off the field, the duo was certainly a Cowboys odd couple, but there was mutual respect for how hard the other worked to win.

> **"Hey, I had it and I needed to wear it."**
>
> [MICHAEL IRVIN]

And there are few others who won as much as Irvin.

THE CIRCUS AND THE RINGMASTER

Irvin's competitive intensity spilled over into his private life. His showmanship on the field sometimes played second fiddle to his audacity off the field, with private parties at Dallas' White House, outrageous accusations, a high-profile arrest, and a shocking fashion statement. Irvin was the poster child for the renegade attitude of "America's Team" in the 1990s; he did what he wanted to do and didn't care about what anyone thought about it. He reveled in the nightlife and benefits that Cowboys blue offered to him—and he took it all in and flaunted it before the media's cameras.

AP/WWP

ABOVE: During his career, the camera-saavy Michael Irvin found himself center stage because of his playing abilities on the field and his extracurricular activities off of it.

That mindset resulted in several brushes with the law. In 1993, when a store clerk in Florida refused to sell Irvin a bottle of wine because the clerk thought Irvin was buying it for a minor, Irvin allegedly jumped behind the counter to serve himself. He also had been accused of assault several times during his career.

But in 1996 on the night before his 30th birthday, the law caught up with Irvin. Irvin and his Cowboys and former University of Miami teammate, Alfredo Roberts, were found in an Irving Residence Inn with a couple of "self-employed" models as well as marijuana, cocaine, and other drug paraphernalia. One of the models, Angela Beck, took the blame for the drugs and was the only person charged.

When the grand jury convened March 26 to discuss Beck's charges, Irvin was told he needed to appear and make a few statements. So Irvin showed up to talk to the grand jury decked out in a get-up—a full-length fur coat—that just begged for insults. Even on an All-Pro, the look wasn't good. It especially wasn't good when Irvin stopped inside and outside the courthouse to sign a few signatures in between testimony. "Hey, I had it," Irvin now says with a smile and at least a hint of remorse, "and I needed to wear it."

A month after the initial arrest, Irvin was also indicted on two drug possession charges.

Irvin eventually pleaded no contest to the charges. He was sentenced to four years probation, fined, and given 800 hours of community service. But his punishment didn't end there. The NFL suspended him for the first five games of the 1996 season, and Irvin lost substantial money in endorsements. A local car dealership sued him for $1.5 million for not being able to perform agreed-upon services in a case that was later settled. Irvin was also pulled from a national Nike campaign.

And that wasn't the last time "The Playmaker" faced charges. On January 3, 1997, 23-year-old Nina Shahravan filed a complaint against Irvin and teammate Erik Williams, accusing Irvin and Williams of sexual assault. KXAS-TV, the Dallas NBC affiliate, was the first to go with the woman's accusations. The accusations came two days before the Cowboys' divisional playoff loss to Carolina, which Irvin missed because of a sprained shoulder.

Shahravan recanted her accusations a few days later, and the charges were dropped. On June 4, 1997, Irvin and Williams filed a lawsuit against the station, eventually settling for $1 million apiece. When asked for reaction to being cleared, Irvin exploded. "I want everyone to report that I have been cleared with the same intensity," Irvin screamed. "Report this with the same intensity as you did the other."

PROLIFIC PLAYMAKER

Irvin's off-the-field transgressions are a frustrating overshadowing of one of the NFL's greatest clutch receivers.

Irvin holds the NFL record for most 100-yard receiving days in a season (11) and consecutive 100-yard days in a year (seven). Both marks were set during the 1995 Super Bowl championship season when Irvin put up a career-high and Cowboys-record 111 receptions and 1,603 yards. That season typified Irvin's career. Even though he had a record-setting number of catches, his 10 touchdowns show how much the Cowboys relied on him to set up other parts of their offense. The team especially relied on "The Playmaker" during the playoffs.

Irvin is the Cowboys' all-time leading postseason receiver in career catches and yards and is tied with Pearson for the most playoff touchdowns. Irvin's 1,315 career postseason yards are good enough for third all-time on the team's total offense charts. He also holds team marks for playoff receptions and yards in a game, both coming in the 1994 NFC Championship Game loss to San Francisco, when Irvin single-handedly kept the Cowboys in the game with 12 grabs for 192 yards.

In the new-era Cowboys' first Super Bowl win in 1992, a 52–17 spanking of Buffalo, Irvin had six catches for 114 yards and two touchdowns, both coming in the second quarter to provide both the relief of early game jitters and the confidence needed to roll to the route. Leading 14–10 with just under two minutes to play in the second quarter, the Cowboys were looking for a momentum swing headed into the half. On the first play after the two-minute warning, Irvin faked his inside slant route and broke outside. Bills corner Nate Odomes had no idea where Irvin was. "The Playmaker" was standing in the back of the end zone with the second of Aikman's four touchdown passes and a 21–10 Cowboys lead.

On Buffalo's first play after the kickoff, Thurman Thomas fumbled to set up the Cowboys at the Bills' 18-yard line. Sensing an opportunity to put the game away, Irvin asked for the ball. He ran an out route that Aikman threw just as Irvin was breaking. The ball found Irvin standing a couple yards away from the end zone. With James Williams draped around his legs, Irvin dove for the goal line, just getting the ball over the line. The touchdown gave Irvin two touchdowns in 18 seconds and Dallas a commanding 28–10 halftime lead.

Those two scores were the only times Irvin saw the end zone during the Cowboys' three Super Bowls in the 1990s. He combined for 10 catches and 142 yards in the next two games. But, contradictory to his well-earned reputation for being brash and outlandish, Irvin didn't have to be spectacular to stand out.

The simple presence and threat of "The Playmaker" explosion was weapon enough.

TOM PIDGEON/GETTY IMAGES

SCRAPE ME UP

Irvin once said that for him to quit playing football he was going to have to be scraped off the field and have his jersey cut off of him.

That's exactly what happened October 10, 1999, at Philadelphia's Veterans Stadium. While running a route he had run, literally, thousands of times, Irvin caught a pass for a nine-yard gain and then ducked his head as he prepared to hit the ground. There wasn't anything particularly vicious about the hit, nothing at all cheap. Irvin dropped the ball and started to get up. No dice. "The Playmaker" couldn't move. In an instant, all that he had worked for, all of the

CRAIG JONES/GETTY IMAGES

ABOVE: Irvin's antics may have given him his bad boy image, but with the end of his playing days has come a change in attitude.

accomplishments, the Super Bowls, the All-Pro selections, the 1,000-yard seasons, the records meant nothing. Irvin couldn't move. He was paralyzed.

Medics from both teams arrived and immediately stabilized Irvin and prepared him for a visit to a spinal trauma center. Eventually, the paralysis wore off, and Irvin was able to move his extremities. However, the 20 minutes he laid on the field were about to change his entire life.

Defensive back Deion Sanders gathered a group of players for prayer. Smith said that looking at Irvin laying on the field makes "all of your deepest fears come to mind." As medical personnel were scraping Irvin off the field, exactly the way he said they were going to have to, a good portion of the almost 67,000 fans in the Vet started cheering an injury that had just ended a man's career.

Irvin remained in Philadelphia for tests and observations. At first, medical staff didn't think the injury to be season-threatening, much less career-threatening. When the results were returned, Irvin was found to have cervical stenosis, a narrowing of the spinal canal. The condition didn't mean

Irvin would get hurt if he continued playing. But, he was told, since the canal is narrower, any trauma to the area could increase the pressure and damage to the injured area. In other words, any major blow to the head could result in paralysis that doesn't go away.

Having been scraped from the field, the jersey was finally cut off July 11, 2000.

ANALYZE THIS

Irvin is still just as opinionated, just as spiffy a dresser and just as loud as he's always been. The intensity just isn't on display on the field anymore. "The Playmaker" is now part of ESPN's *NFL Countdown* and other ESPN-related NFL programming. It's a job he couldn't get when he first retired.

After Irvin announced his retirement, he was set to work for FOX in the 2000 season. However, more legal problems surfaced and FOX didn't want to deal with the hassle.

After FOX fell through, Irvin started making amends with local media. He began doing radio and television shows, trying to build a reputation in another arena. He also started devoting more time to T.D. Jakes's Potter's House Ministries in Dallas, something Sanders turned Irvin on to late in both of their careers.

Slowly, the jobs started coming Irvin's way. FOX allowed him to stop by periodically on *The Best Damn Sports Show Period.* The Dallas Desperados Arena League team, which is owned by the Cowboys, let him work their local broadcasts. That led to a studio gig for NBC's national Arena League coverage and, eventually, to his current studio analyst position, first at ESPN and now at NFL Network.

While preparing to cover the NFL draft for ESPN at the start of his time there, one of the producers of ESPN's coverage said Irvin had found his niche because he "takes it very seriously. He studies, he prepares, he knows what is going on, and he's very good at it because he wants to be the best." Ah, "The Playmaker" lives.

TROY
AIKMAN

Troy Aikman walked into his introductory news conference the day after the 1989 NFL draft and made only one promise. For every win, his high school in Henrietta, Oklahoma, and UCLA would get a $1,000 donation.

If folks in those two places were relying on that promise, there was a lot of starving going on. The blond-locked UCLA quarterback arrived in Dallas as the first draft pick of the Jerry Jones-Jimmy Johnson regime. He would be the foundation of three Super Bowl champions, become one of the most accurate passers in NFL history, a Hall of Famer, and a city legend.

But, first, he had to take a legendary beating. The off season before Aikman's first year, Jones and Johnson presented their new poster boy to anyone who wanted to see him. He had just signed the largest rookie contract in history, and Aikman was making the Cowboys' sales pitch to every local business, group, family dinner, wherever, that would give the trio a chance to explain why 1989 Cowboys season tickets were a good idea. Listening to Jones, the pitch wasn't very convincing. On the day he handed Aikman the keys to the Cowboys' franchise, even Jones wasn't really sure what he had done. "It is with reserved enthusiasm," Jones said at the news conference, "that I announce Troy Aikman has signed to be the quarterback of the future."

As the first pick in the 1989 draft, all of the Jones-Johnson hopes were pinned on Aikman. He had started his college career at Oklahoma as a much-ballyhooed local kid who decided to run Barry Switzer's Wishbone. That didn't last long as Aikman broke his leg his first season, gave way to Sooners legend Jamel Holloway, and went west to UCLA. As a senior, Aikman finished third in the Heisman Trophy balloting behind cross-town rival and his future Cowboys backup, Rodney Peete of USC, and Oklahoma State's Barry Sanders.

That's about where the good times ended.

> **"It is with reserved enthusiasm that I announce Troy Aikman has signed to be the quarterback of the future."**
>
> [JERRY JONES]

The Cowboys opened 1989 with a 28–0 loss in New Orleans. It was closer the next week 27–21 against Atlanta. Then, the whipping started. Five straight double-digit losses, including a 30–13 loss to the New York Giants in which Aikman suffered a fractured left index finger that needed surgery. He returned six weeks later, but in the cruelest of twists, missed the Cowboys' only win of the year by one week.

Dallas finished 1–15 in 1989 and 7–9 the next year. Aikman was earning his NFL stripes, taking his lickings, getting right back up, and trying to keep on ticking. The 7–9 record in 1990 had fans thinking the playoffs might be on the 1991 horizon. The Philadelphia Eagles crushed those thoughts under a mountain of humanity, giving Aikman a monumental beating.

TROY AIKMAN

Born: November 21, 1966, West Covina, California
Position: Quarterback
Years with the Cowboys: 1989–2000
All-Pro/Pro Bowl Appearances: 4/6
Honors:
* No. 1 pick in the 1989 draft
* Super Bowl XXVII MVP
* NFL rookie record: 379 yards passing against the Phoenix Cardinals
* NFL playoff record: 94-yard touchdown pass (1994)
* Cowboys record: 4,715 career attempts
* Cowboys record: 2,898 career completions
* Cowboys record: 32,942 career passing yards
* Cowboys record: 165 career touchdown passes
* Cowboys record: 61.5 career completion percentage
* Cowboys record: 156 passing attempts without an interception
* Winningest quarterback of any decade in NFL history (90 wins in the 1990s)
* Only quarterback to win three out of four Super Bowls; one of three quarterbacks to win three Super Bowls
* Inducted into the Pro Football Hall of Fame in 2006
* Inducted into the Ring of Honor in 2005

In a 24–0 loss in Week 3, Philadelphia sacked Aikman 11 times for 67 yards in losses. The Cowboys had such a hard time stopping Clyde Simmons, Jerome Brown, Mike Pitts, Mike Golic, Reggie White, and Seth Joyner that they committed a pass interference penalty and had two holding penalties. The Eagles also picked Aikman off three times. "It was just one of those days," a dazed Aikman said after the game.

During the Super Bowl years, Aikman reaped the rewards of one of the greatest offensive lines ever assembled. Has there ever been anyone—other than those starving souls from 1989—who deserved it more?

IN THE FOG

San Francisco quarterback Steve Young and Aikman were the sheriffs in a few playoff shootouts in the 1990s. As the century turned and two great franchises prepared for the afterlife without their great leaders, Young and Aikman became linked more for what was happening to their brains than anything either was doing on the field.

Young and Aikman led their teams to Super Bowl wins in the 1990s, both picking up a Super Bowl MVP trophy. The two famed gunslingers that played in three straight memorable NFC Championship games against one another from 1992 to 1994 are also part of a long list of quarterbacks rushed into retirement because of the violent nature of their industry.

Aikman suffered four concussions in his last 20 NFL starts, 10 total in his career. Although tough as nails, he didn't play a full year after 1997. Still, even after a brutal 2000 season, Aikman wanted to stick around for more. The Cowboys had taken Quincy Carter in the 2001 draft and were prepared to let the rookie, like Aikman did in 1989, learn on the job. Aikman was told the Cowboys were probably going in a different direction and that he was free to look around. At that point, most figured Aikman would simply retire to the broadcast booth, where executives were salivating to get their hands on the articulate, insightful eye candy who had football credibility.

He eventually packed his bags for FOX, but that didn't mean he still wasn't looking. Kansas City, San Diego, and Miami each inquired about Aikman suiting up for them. He seriously considered leaving, before he got a history lesson and a phone call.

Aikman remembered Tony Dorsett's Denver years. He wasn't in the league yet, but he remembered seeing a legendary Cowboys figure spend the twilight of his career as nothing more than a shadow of the Hall of Famer he turned out to be. Then, the most legendary of all Cowboys players, Roger

Staubach, called. Staubach made it to age 38 before retiring because of a total of, Staubach estimated, 12 to 14 concussions over his playing career. The two talked about legacy and about logic. "When you're an athlete, you have that drive to want to continue to compete," Staubach said. "But, there is a time to retire and that is a decision that you have to evaluate individually."

Aikman never played a game after the 2000 season, but he did have the desire. He structured his FOX contract so that if he felt a good enough offer came his way, he could leave the booth and let his new buddies call his games rather than watch them with him.

Former Washington Redskins quarterback-turned broadcaster Joe Theismann, who was forced to retire after Lawrence Taylor treated his leg like a twig in the nastiest football injury ever broadcast, had the same kind of loophole in his deals well into his 40s. "Players just don't think about retirement," former New York Giants quarterback and CBS broadcaster Phil Simms said.

Unless, like Young and Aikman, two certain Hall of Famers, they are forced to.

UNRAVELING

Aikman played five series of the Cowboys' first three games of the 2000 season after suffering yet another concussion. He came back to start a 41–24 home loss against San Francisco and got booed. Two weeks later in the Meadowlands it got worse, giving more steam to the train that was taking Aikman toward retirement. It was the worst game of his career in the worst season of his career. He tied a team record with five interceptions in the 19–14 loss. He had entered the game as one of the lowest-rated quarterbacks in the league. Five picks lowered the rating even further and, as is always popular in Dallas, started cries for backup Randall Cunningham. "The thing that has driven me to compete each year and in each game," Aikman said after the loss, "is to gain the respect of my teammates. If I didn't have that, then it would be disappointing. But if I continue to have performances like this, then that's what will happen."

Aikman finished 2000 ranked last among NFL starters in quarterback rating. His 64.3 rating was the second lowest of his career, the worst being the

1–15 year in 1989. His 1,632 yards and seven touchdowns were the fewest in his 12 seasons.

THE LAST PLAY

Throughout Aikman's Dallas career, Cowboys fans became as familiar with concussion terms as they did with blitzing terms. They knew which neurosurgeons were going to get quoted and knew as much about CAT scans as they did the St. Louis Rams. They had seen their leader lay unconscious on the field. Fans held their collective breaths when No. 8 went down. Would this be the one that puts him out for good?

Concussions have a lingering effect. A person who suffers one is four times more likely, according to studies, to have another one. And when your business is beating someone else's brains out, well, those percentages tend to increase.

The 2000 season was Dave Campo's first as Cowboys head coach. Aikman had championed the change from Chan Gailey and was back for a 12th season. However, the team was going through a personality crisis and was having a hard time deciding if they would try to hold on to a glorious past or make the necessary changes to compete in what had became a very different NFL. While the Cowboys were deciding, Dallas suffered their first of three straight 5–11 seasons. Aikman was only around for the first. And, even then, he was only around for a few games. He missed parts of six games with concussion effects and a back injury he later confessed was worse in the long term than he first thought.

During the first quarter of a 32–13 Dallas win over Washington, the Cowboys had third and goal at the Washington one-yard line. Aikman slid out of the pocket and drifted toward the right sideline. A sold-out Texas Stadium crowd silently rose. Aikman was on the run but still looking to put the ball in the end zone. As Aikman got closer to the right sideline, rookie linebacker LaVar Arrington, who probably had posters in his bedroom of Aikman, Smith, and Irvin as a kid, blasted Aikman as he released the ball, sending Aikman

LEFT: Troy Aikman took a beating both at the beginning and end of his stellar career.

flying toward the bench area. "He wasn't supposed to get all the way outside," said Campo. "It was a play-action pass. They covered, and he had to scramble."

"I don't know, unless he just got real clearance, that he will play again this season," Cowboys owner Jerry Jones said after the game.

Aikman never played again.

FAREWELL

It is one of the most glorious of positions in sport. The title of Dallas Cowboys quarterback carries enormous pressure, but it also carries major reward. Win in this town, and you will be a deity. Lose and your carcass will be sent up the river. Or at least to Oklahoma.

The latest of the Cowboys' franchise quarterbacks was an Oklahoma good ole boy turned UCLA pretty boy turned "America's Team" golden boy. He recovered from severe beatings his first three seasons to emerge as the MVP of the Cowboys' first Super Bowl win in the 1990s. He brought two more of those Lombardi Trophies to town while building a Hall of Fame career.

Troy Aikman's statistics were never overly impressive. They didn't have to be. With Michael Irvin on the outside, Emmitt Smith in your backfield on his way to becoming the all-time leading rusher in NFL history, and a defense that demolished people, Dallas needed a corporate manager. They got one of the highest order in Aikman. He was as demanding on his teammates as coach Jimmy Johnson was. Aikman was the ultimate tactician, precisely perfect for what the Cowboys were trying to do. Aikman ran offensive coordinator Norv Turner's timing offense flawlessly. Actually, there wasn't a lot of running to do. For as much credit as Dallas got for being innovative during The Triplets years, the offense was based on Smith opening up the passing game, Aikman softening defenses with quick, underneath throws to Irvin and tight end Jay Novacek and then the occasional jugular toss to Alvin Harper. In fact, one season the Cowboys called the same lead draw play to Smith more than 300 times.

That's the way those early 1990s Dallas teams were. Johnson knew his talent was better than yours. He knew Aikman would out-accurate your guy. He knew Smith would outgain your back, Irvin out-talk, out-perform, and out-party anyone on your team. The Triplets were three individuals, but the sum of their parts made the Cowboys one hell of a whole.

For his career, Aikman never finished as the conference or league leader in passing. He made his millions in management, valuing quality over quantity. During the 1991 season, the Cowboys were sitting at 6–5, with their playoff hopes fading and a game in Washington against the 11–0 Redskins looming. Aikman sprained his knee on the first play of the second half and missed the rest of the game. Before he left, Aikman was part of a Dallas team that recovered an onside kick in the second quarter and went for it three times on fourth down. The first of those attempts was a fourth and five from Washington's 33-yard line. Aikman hit Irvin for six yards, nothing fancy, but exactly what the team needed. It was enough to get the Redskins thinking that this young team wasn't impressed with the 11-game winning streak. Still on their heels, Smith busted through the Redskins' secondary for a 32-yard touchdown run on third and 15 for the Cowboys' first touchdown. The series was a perfect example of Aikman precision and the unique firepower each of The Triplets provided.

> ## "He wasn't supposed to get all the way outside. It was a play-action pass. They covered, and he had to scramble."
>
> [DAVE CAMPO]

On the last play of the half, Dallas faced yet another fourth-down situation. This time, Aikman didn't go to Irvin. Instead, he threw to the corner of the end zone and made a jump ball out of what would be his final throw of the game. The Redskins had two defenders in the area, but the Cowboys had a former SEC high-jump champion on their side. Harper picked the ball out of the air for a 34-yard touchdown and a 14–7 halftime lead. Three weeks later, Dallas wiped the worn-out Veterans Stadium turf with the Eagles and clinched the team's first playoff spot since 1985.

Aikman missed the final four regular-season games and the wild card win over Chicago in Soldier Field. He played poorly in relief of Steve Beuerlein in the divisional game against Detroit, but the stage had been set. The Cowboys had arrived as a contender and Aikman as their leader. The next season started the run of three Super Bowls in four years.

From 1991 to 1996, Aikman's worst completion percentage was 63.7 percent in 1996. During the 1993 season, widely considered Dallas' best team of that era,

"An earthquake in Santa Monica tonight is the only thing that's going to stop Dallas."

[JAMES LOFTON]

Aikman set a team record by connecting on 69.1 percent of his tosses. During the playoffs, he had a ridiculous stretch of three straight games where he completed 80 percent. That season, Aikman threw for 3,100 yards, 15 touchdowns, and six interceptions. Statistically, his best season was 1992 when he threw for 3,445 yards and 23 touchdowns. The Cowboys beat Buffalo 52–17 in the Super Bowl for Dallas' first title in 15 years. Aikman, the MVP, was simply spotless. He completed 22 of 30 balls for 273 yards and four touchdowns and was not picked off. "An earthquake in Santa Monica tonight," Bills receiver James Lofton said after watching Aikman pick his team apart, "is the only thing that's going to stop Dallas."

Actually, organizational infighting and Aikman getting his head rattled finally led to Dallas' decline. The Cowboys won the Super Bowl again the next season, but then the well-chronicled Jerry Jones-Jimmy Johnson feud put Jimmy on a boat in the Florida Keys and led to Jones hiring Aikman's first college coach.

By that point, Aikman had his routines. So did Irvin. So did Smith. So did Moose Johnston. So did Mark Stepnoski. So did Harper. So did the defense. Barry Switzer was told to leave things alone, which is exactly what he did.

Aikman led the Cowboys back to the 1994 NFC Championship Game in Switzer's first year, but he had his worst statistical season since 1990. His completion percentage was still very high (64.5 percent), but his yards fell to 2,676, and his 13 touchdowns were countered by 12 interceptions. He threw three picks in the 38–28 NFC Championship Game loss in San Francisco. One of the interceptions was returned for a touchdown, one of three 49ers scores in the first five minutes. Despite the 21–0 hole, Dallas climbed back on a muddy Candlestick Park track. Aikman hit Irvin 12 times for 192 yards, the receptions tying a championship game record and the yardage setting a new one. He did turn the ball over, but Aikman was a stud, throwing for 380 yards against a defense that knocked him down 19 times.

Late in the game, the Cowboys had a chance to claw back fully and cut the lead to three. Aikman threw a ball toward Irvin deep in 49ers territory. Then-San Francisco cornerback Deion Sanders pushed his buddy but didn't get called for interference on a play that looked eerily similar to a play earlier in the game when Larry Brown was called for interfering with Jerry Rice. That play set up a San Francisco touchdown. Not getting the same call to go their way set off Switzer. He bumped an official and got called for a 15-yard penalty, and defensive end Charles Haley retired. "This was very frustrating," Aikman said sitting in his locker after the game. "It was my first playoff loss as a starter. We came in here as the champs and are until proven otherwise. It just got proven otherwise today."

A month later, Switzer was eating hot dogs on the sidelines as coach of the NFC Pro Bowl team. Switzer's approach never sat well with Aikman, but there really wasn't a whole lot Switzer could do. Jones changed only the head coach after the second Super Bowl. In his second season, Switzer got more comfortable around the players and his built-in assistants. The Cowboys

BELOW: Aikman was the meticulous leader of the dominant Cowboys teams of the 1990s.

BRIAN BAHR/GETTY IMAGES

responded, beating Pittsburgh in the Super Bowl.

That is the last time Dallas has been to the promised land. Switzer was gone two years later in favor of Steelers offensive coordinator Chan Gailey. The two-year experiment was a disaster for Aikman. The go-to receiver the team traded for, Joey Galloway, shattered his knee in the first game of the 1999 season. Aikman's completion percentage slipped under 60 percent, and his yardage totals suffered in Gailey's multiple sets. The retirement scene was being rehearsed.

In Dallas, a legend's sendoff is often as remembered as the player. There was the tearful Staubach retirement and, just a year earlier when Irvin left the game, the exit of the first Triplet. Aikman's final goodbye would have emotion, tears, and all the memories. Even if the actual release was hastily planned.

In March 2001, Aikman was due a $7 million roster bonus that would have extended his deal through 2007. Jones had already determined that, in this salary cap era, the team needed to cut ties with its franchise quarterback. He just didn't know how quickly it needed to be done. A clause in Aikman's contract made it necessary for Jones to either waive him or extend the deadline by "the seventh day after the start of the league season," which was March 2, 2001. Everyone thought that meant things needed to be in place by the following Thursday. However, a league official told Jones that, to be safe, everything needed to be solved that Wednesday. The Cowboys quickly sent Aikman's agent, Leigh Steinberg, an urgent fax. The two sides worked together and, in a span of 90 minutes, Troy Aikman was no longer a Dallas Cowboy.

> **"I've seen Danny White retire. Tom Rafferty and Ed Jones and Michael Irvin and Daryl Johnston and Jay Novacek, and you think your time will never come."**
>
> [TROY AIKMAN]

The tearful farewell came a month later. "I've seen Danny White retire. Tom Rafferty and Ed Jones and Michael Irvin and Daryl Johnston and Jay Novacek, and you think your time will never come," a weeping Aikman told a giant gathering at the Stadium Club at Texas Stadium. "My time has come. Today I announce my retirement from the National Football League and the Dallas Cowboys."

Aikman talked about watching Bob Lilly, Lee Roy Jordan, Staubach, Tony Dorsett, and Randy White while growing up. He talked about being able to live out a dream by putting on the Cowboys' uniform.

Then, he addressed Smith and Irvin, who were both in the crowd. Tears streaming, he talked about the special relationship he had with Irvin. One a country boy from Henrietta, Oklahoma, the other the son of a roofer from inner-city Miami, the duo was the oddest of Cowboys odd couples. During Irvin's darkest hours in 1996, Aikman stood behind his buddy, risking a lot in public image to show up at one of Irvin's trials to support "The Playmaker." Irvin said he will never forget the gesture.

Aikman then turned to Smith and lamented that he wouldn't be the quarterback that handed the ball to Smith when he broke the all-time rushing record. "We were The Triplets," Aikman said, "and I loved it."

Aikman left the Cowboys as one of the most decorated quarterbacks in NFL history. His legacy is one of accuracy and guts. He took an absolute beating in 1989 and 1990 when the team was just laying the foundation for their dynasty. Almost every passing record is his, and they are not likely to be broken. Always most dangerous in the playoffs, Aikman completed 64 percent of his passes in the postseason. He had four games where he completed at least 12 passes in a row.

Along with Irvin, he also served as a bridge from the old Cowboys to the new. He was the first draft pick in the Jones-Johnson era. He didn't play under Tom Landry and Tex Schramm or with Dorsett and White like Irvin did, but he played with Ed "Too Tall" Jones, took the beating for the 1–15 1989 team, and was around when the Herschel Walker trade was made, a move that eventually brought Smith to town. "I used to joke with Roger Staubach all of the time," Aikman told the *Dallas Morning News* not long after he was released, "about what it was going to be like when nobody care[s] about me." In this town, that doesn't happen to deities.

EMMITT
SMITH

Troy Aikman was having to make adjustments, but he wasn't about to ask Emmitt Smith to take a seat. The Cowboys running back was so banged up that Aikman was having to squat to give Smith the ball at a lower angle. With the way Smith was going during this game against the Giants in the Meadowlands, Aikman would have crawled through embers and ashes to give Smith the ball.

The Cowboys and New York Giants had battled all season for the 1993 NFC East title, home field advantage, and a bye week. Smith gave them all three with one of the gutsiest performances in Dallas history. He touched the ball a team-record 42 times, going for 168 yards on the ground on 32 carries and wrapping up his third straight rushing title along the way. He hauled in 10 Aikman passes for another 61 yards. He also scored Dallas' only touchdown in a 16–13 overtime win.

The numbers were impressive, but the conditions even more so. In the second quarter, Smith got lost in the Giants' secondary for 46 yards. When Greg Jackson brought Smith down, Smith felt Jackson fall hard on his shoulder. Smith jogged to the sidelines with his right arm dangling limp. He rested two snaps and then returned to the huddle. When he got there, Smith looked his offensive line in the eyes and said that someone had better be running right behind him for the rest of the game. He was going to tote the note, but he needed friendlies behind him to pick up the pieces.

On the fall, Smith had separated his shoulder. The seriousness of the injury gets worse as the years go by. Before he retires, Smith will get asked why his right arm looks so natural. Someone will ask, "It's not true that you lost it in that game against the Giants in the 1993 season?" Of the three degrees of separation, this was the least serious. But, how non-serious can any shoulder be if it's separated?

When Smith showed up on the sidelines, trainer Kevin O'Neill immediately knew what was wrong. He also knew what answer he was going to get from the All-Pro. Smith wanted back in, and O'Neill needed to fix it on the spot. Smith didn't have time for an injury. O'Neill grabbed a thigh pad and put it under Smith's shoulder pads for extra protection. Then, he winced as the Cowboys running back went back in to run the football.

After he got hurt, Smith caught seven passes and ran the ball 19 times. Before he went down, Smith and Aikman were dissecting the team that ended up with the NFC's second-best record. Aikman was on his way to his second straight game with an 80 percent completion percentage. By halftime, Smith had 109 yards and the Cowboys were up 13–0. When the team got to the locker room, trainers took a detailed look. They didn't say he couldn't play, but they weren't rushing to saddle the horse back up. Smith did that himself. "I had to make a decision at halftime," Smith said afterward. "It was pretty rough. I came here with every intention of doing whatever was needed to win. I wanted to keep playing."

After David Treadwell tied the game with a 31-yard field goal with 10 seconds left to push Dallas to overtime, Smith grabbed his helmet. Coach Jimmy Johnson walked over to Smith and asked how much more juice he had. "Play me until I can't play anymore," Smith said.

After the Giants were forced to punt, Aikman bent down to his backfield mate and gave him the ball. And kept giving him the ball. Smith was still playing, so Johnson was letting him go. On one play, Smith spun one defender down and picked up 10 yards. Johnson told backup Lincoln Coleman to get in the game. "And," Coleman said, "Emmitt told me to get out."

In total, Smith picked up 41 of the 52 yards Dallas needed on the drive to put Eddie Murray in range for a 41-yard field goal attempt. Murray drilled the kick. The Cowboys now had home field advantage and a bye. And the city had a new hero.

The win gave Smith, who was so sore after the game that he had to have help getting dressed, two full weeks off. The Giants were forced to play a first-round wildcard game against Minnesota, which

EMMITT SMITH

Born: May 15, 1969, in Pensacola, Florida
Position: Running Back
Years with the Cowboys: 1990–2002
All-Pro/Pro Bowl Appearances: 4/9
Honors:
* Four-time NFL rushing title holder
* Named NFL's Offensive Rookie of the Year in 1990
* NFL MVP in 1993
* Super Bowl XXVIII MVP
* NFL record: 17,418 total yards rushing
* NFL record: 153 all-time rushing touchdowns
* NFL record: 11 seasons of more than 1,000 yards rushing
* NFL record: Five straight seasons of more than 1,400 yards rushing (first-ever)
* Inducted into the Pro Football Hall of Fame in 2010
* Inducted into the Ring of Honor in 2005

they won. However, the Dallas loss put New York in San Francisco for their divisional playoff game, where the Giants got steamrolled 44–3.

The Cowboys dispatched those same 49ers a week later and won their second consecutive Super Bowl over the Bills exactly four weeks to the day the team was forced to fight a battle with its best gunslinger as no more than a one-armed bandit.

That was still more firepower than any other team in the league.

YOU LOOK FAMILIAR

When Smith arrived at Valley Ranch for the first time, Cowboys quarterback Troy Aikman thought the Florida running back looked familiar. "I played against that guy," Aikman said, trying to figure out where he had seen the man that would spend the next decade behind him, "in the Aloha Bowl. That was his freshman year, the year he came in and set the world on fire."

During his freshman year, Smith went for more than 1,000 yards by the seventh game of the year, breaking the record of a guy who had recently taken off from Dallas, Tony Dorsett. That same year, he joined another Cowboy, Herschel Walker, as the only freshman to finish in the top 10 in the Heisman race.

Smith only stayed three years at Florida, but he set almost 60 school records, including most career yards. For most of his tenure, he played for a team ravaged by scholarship limits. Had he not, running backs coach Joe Brodsky said at the time, "There is no telling what that guy would have done. In his last year, he was playing with a small deficiency up front and he didn't back down."

As the 1990 draft approached, coach Jimmy Johnson was trying to make a move up. The Cowboys had traded for running back Terrence Flagler three days earlier, but Smith was certainly on their radar screens. Johnson was familiar with Smith, having tried to recruit him to Miami when Johnson was a Hurricane and Smith was a standout at Escambia High near Pensacola.

Dallas didn't have its own first-round pick, having used it in the supplemental draft to take Johnson pupil Steve Walsh of Miami. They did have

Minnesota's first-round pick from the Herschel Walker trade. Wanting speed and size on defense, Johnson was trying to use the pick to trade up for Baylor linebacker James Francis. When Francis went to Cincinnati at No. 12, Johnson knew he just needed to get ahead of Green Bay and Atlanta to get Smith. The Jets had taken Penn State's Blair Thomas with the second pick in the draft. At No. 18, the second running back was taken when Johnson got his man. Green Bay was left with Darrell Thompson, and the Falcons got Steve Broussard.

When he got to Dallas, fans saw the small, stocky frame and immediately began to think Tony Dorsett The Sequel had arrived. Smith is actually shorter than Dorsett, but few running backs have ever had Smith's raw, lower-body power. "I'm not going to say I can come in and do wonders for the Cowboys," Smith said the day of his first Cowboys' practice. "I will tell you that I'll do the best I can."

On the day he was drafted, one coach told the *Dallas Morning News*: "They'll find Emmitt doesn't have as pure a speed as they'd like and he's a little guy, so when he gets hurt, he's in trouble."

Smith, like Dorsett, never really did get hurt, playing in 201 of a possible 209 games in his Dallas career. He broke Dorsett's team rushing record in his ninth season, and his season mark his third year in the league.

As it turned out, Smith wasn't Dorsett The Sequel. He was Emmitt Smith Part One.

THE HUMP GAME

It took 11 years and a new generation of stars, but it finally happened. The Cowboys swaggered into Candlestick Park in San Francisco January 17, 1993, and took back the torch many thought they lent to the 49ers that day in 1982 when Joe Montana ripped out Dallas fans' hearts and Dwight Clark tap-danced on them.

Just like The Catch game, Dallas's 30–20 win in San Francisco that day signaled a changing of the guard, a banner handover from the team of the 1980s to the one that would carry the 1990s. The win put the Cowboys in its first Super Bowl under the Jerry Jones-Jimmy Johnson watch. Dallas hadn't been to a Super Bowl in 13 years, after getting to five in the game's first 13 years.

The team was going this time because of ballsy calls from Johnson, big plays from big-time players, and an adjustment over morning coffee. Johnson got up in the predawn hours to check the weather. When he looked out his window to see rain soaking San Francisco, he gathered the staff to discuss changes he wanted to make. He wanted to be even more aggressive, especially early, in case conditions worsened later. The Cowboys needed to get their licks in early.

The weather ended up not being a factor, but the Cowboys' aggressive game plan was. Tied at the half, Dallas put together a 78-yard drive and two 79-yarders in the second half to seal the game. One of the 79-yarders came after Johnson showed his brashness by trying to close the coffin with seven minutes to play. Instead of kicking a field goal on fourth and one from the 49ers' seven-yard line, which would have put Dallas up 14, Johnson tried Smith up the middle. Smith was buried. San Francisco turned around and marched 93 yards to pull within four at 24–20.

The Cowboys got the ball back with just over four minutes left. Again trying to be aggressive, Johnson had Smith stay in to block on first down. Aikman dropped back and hit Alvin Harper coming over the middle. He wasn't stopped until he reached the San Francisco nine-yard line. On the next play, Aikman hit Kelvin Martin for the nail that Johnson had been looking for the drive earlier. "A lot of people would have been conservative in that situation," 49ers coach George Seifert said after the game. "They took chances, and it worked for them."

It was a typical game for Smith. He led everyone with 173 total yards, doing it with another 100-yard game and mixing in receptions designed to simply let him get in the open field and do his thing. He scored Dallas' first touchdown and found paydirt again in the fourth quarter on a 16-yard pass from Aikman. Smith, who ran for more than 100 yards in each of the Cowboys' playoff games that year, finished with 114 rushing yards, but was contained early on because of San Francisco's determination that he wasn't going to beat them.

Smith did anyway. This game and the Super Bowl win two weeks later over Buffalo defined this new breed of silver and blue champions. They didn't care what you did. They lined up and kicked you in the teeth, and if you stopped them, that was fine. Eventually they would wear you down with ungodly defensive line depth and a runner that chipped and chipped at your defense until you finally broke.

And, make no mistake, Smith made many a defense buckle.

AWOL EMMITT

Before he was able to forever cement his place in Cowboys history, Smith first had to take care of Smith. After the Cowboys won the first Super Bowl after the 1992 season, Smith let owner Jerry Jones know that $465,000 wasn't the going rate for a guy that had twice led the league in rushing and was coming off a year in which he set the franchise record. Smith said he would like a contract that would make him a long-time Cowboy and one that paid him right around what the Buffalo Bills' Thurman Thomas was raking in. In fact, it was Thomas who was causing all these problems. After the Cowboys' win over Buffalo in the Super Bowl the year before, Thomas ran Smith down and told him: "A pay day is headed your way. Go get your money!"

The sides bickered all through a training camp that Smith missed. As the season approached, Jones and coach Jimmy Johnson still weren't overly concerned. Smith wasn't likely going to play much in preseason, and, from all accounts, he was staying in shape. With Smith tucked away at his own personal training camp, the team kept chugging and Emmitt and Jerry kept battling.

The season opener was a Monday nighter in Washington's RFK Stadium. A major rivalry game and the Cowboys were staring at the fact that Alabama rookie Derrick Lassic was about to be their starter.

When the Redskins walked all over the defending Super Bowl champions 35–16, Jones tried not to get nervous. He figured Smith would get enough pressure from teammates and that, eventually, he would see that the money wasn't that far off. Dallas had three games before their first bye week. Jones set a personal goal of having Smith ready to go for the game against Green Bay at Texas Stadium after the week off.

ABOVE: Smith's storied career with Dallas includes breaking the sacred NFL all-time rushing record.

Before playing Buffalo in Week 2, Jones gave himself a history lesson. He found that no team had ever started a season 0–2 and come back to win the Super Bowl. This Cowboys team had just won one and to a man who thought his team would be even better in 1993, Jones tried not to let history affect his judgment, but he was aware of the numbers.

When Buffalo bounced Dallas in Texas Stadium the next week 13–10, Jones admitted his negotiating power had been severely limited. The two sides hadn't talked for two days until Jones's phone rang Monday morning. Both sides made proposals. Four days later, less than three days from a game in Phoenix and after a very strange Wednesday conference call that included Smith's mother, Mary, the two sides signed a contract in Atlanta in the afternoon and flew to Dallas that night.

Smith stepped off Jones's jet, raised his arms in triumph, and got the applause of a crowd that had been begging to see their franchise back in action.

Smith did get his money, $13.6 million over four years with $2 million paid up front in a check Jones handed to Smith personally. "When he signs his contract for four years, then the Cowboys are big winners," Jones said at an evening news conference at Texas Stadium. "And when I sign this bonus check . . . he's a winner."

Both sides did turn out fine that year. The Cowboys get their second straight Super Bowl title, and Smith, again, led the league in rushing despite missing those first two games. He made up for the lost time in one game when he ran for 237 yards in a Halloween win over the Philadelphia Eagles, the highest NFL total in 16 years. Later against Phoenix, he grabbed an 86-yard reception from Bernie Kosar, who was subbing for an injured Troy Aikman. The pass is still one of the team's top 10 longest pass plays.

Dallas finished the season with eight straight wins, including Smith's memorable performance against the Giants. In the Super Bowl, again against Buffalo, he ran for 91 yards and two touchdowns in the second half. He finished with 132 yards, the second straight year he had gone more than 100 yards in the Super Bowl, and won MVP honors.

Smith was the consensus league MVP. It wasn't his biggest rushing year, but he had proven there was no other back more valuable. And the Cowboys had him locked up for three more years.

ONE MORE RUN

It was one of the more bizarre divorces in NFL history. Jimmy Johnson wins two straight Super Bowls after leading the team from the depths of the first post-Tom Landry years and gets fired in favor of a former college coach who, by his own admission, was doing little before "Jerry called me to get off my couch in Norman."

Johnson out, former Oklahoma legend Barry Switzer in. Johnson was hurt that Jones had blabbered at an NFL meeting in Orlando that 500 coaches could coach the Cowboys' talented roster to a Super Bowl title.

Switzer must not have been one of the 500 because even though the Cowboys made it to the NFC Championship Game in 1994, Switzer's team didn't make it to the Super Bowl.

That means Jones was even more determined the next season that Switzer could do it. Jones grabbed one of the 49ers' biggest weapons from the year before, Deion Sanders, and stuck him in the Cowboys' secondary. He had Emmitt, Troy, and Michael back and now, with "Prime Time," it was time to prove to Jimmy Johnson and the rest of the NFL world that Jones could win one without Jimmy.

Although Aikman didn't appreciate Switzer's laid-back ways, Smith didn't take much issue with him. As long as Switzer kept feeding the monster, Smith was fine. He carried the ball more in 1995 than any other time in his career. He also put up the most yards of his career, breaking his own team record with 1,773 yards and besting John Riggins's 12-year-old NFL mark by rushing for 25 touchdowns.

In the playoffs, it was The Triplets doing their thing. In an NFC Championship Game win over Green Bay, Aikman threw for 255 yards and two touchdowns, both to Irvin, and Smith ran for 150 yards and three touchdowns, his best career playoff totals in both categories.

The next week the Cowboys popped Pittsburgh 27–17 to win their third Super Bowl in four years. Smith didn't have a great game, but he did have a great year. He was the first non-kicker to lead the league in scoring since Jerry Rice in 1987. He led the league in rushing for the fourth and final time. He was also tops in carries, rushing touchdowns, and total touchdowns.

BOWING OUT

The 1995 season wasn't the last hurrah for Smith or the Cowboys, but it was the beginning of the end. The Cowboys snuck in the playoffs in 1996 but lost the divisional game at Carolina. One year and a 6–10 record later and

Switzer was back on his couch in Oklahoma. In was Chan Gailey, who tried to run a sophisticated, multiple formation look that ended up alienating most players, especially quarterback Troy Aikman. The Cowboys made the playoffs in both of Gailey's years but were embarrassingly knocked out by the Arizona Cardinals at home after Gailey's first year. Two years of Gailey and at the request of Aikman among others, Gailey was gone.

Dave Campo, the secondary coach and then defensive coordinator for Jimmy Johnson's great teams, took over as the calendar turned to a new century. By this time, talk began swirling around whether Smith could hold up and break Walter Payton's all-time rushing mark. After slumps, at least in terms of Smith's regular production, during Switzer's final two years, Smith actually had nice success in the Gailey era, finishing in the top five in the league in rushing yards in 1998 and 1999.

Coming into the year, Smith was sitting at just under 14,000 career yards, about 2,800 yards short of Payton's record. Despite Dallas' recent struggles, Smith had still rushed for more than 1,000 yards nine straight years.

In 2000, the team was bad, playing its first season without Irvin and putting up its first of three straight 5–11 seasons. However, Smith was not. He kept his 1,000-yard season streak alive rushing for 1,203.

The next season, the Cowboys were again minus one of The Triplets, when concussions sent Aikman to the broadcast booth. Dallas was bad again but, again, Smith extended his streak, this time to an NFL record 11 straight seasons. He finished with 1,021 yards and, going into 2002, stood less than 540 yards from one of football's most storied records.

Having finished with only 10 wins in the last two years, Campo was feeling the heat. He needed to show some sort of improvement, or Jones would be looking for a new figurehead. Because Jones fired Johnson in early 1994, the most tired sports talk show question had been, "When is Jerry going to get a football man in here and give him control?" The answer was not yet. Jones wanted Smith to break the record as a Cowboy, and he didn't care if the team pulled a season like 1989 to do it.

Dallas opened 2002 in the absolute worst possible way. The Cowboys went down I-45 and christened Houston's new Reliant Stadium by giving the expansion Houston Texans a gift victory in their first-ever game. Smith rushed

ABOVE: With a methodical style, Smith grabbed every Cowboys rushing record and four NFL marks.

for 67 yards, his best game for a month. Seven weeks into the season and Smith still hadn't gotten the 539 yards he needed to break the record.

Finally, in Week 9 against Seattle in Texas Stadium, Smith reached the NFL's Holy Grail. In a game pitting a 1–5 Seahawks team and a 3–4 Cowboys team, a sold-out stadium wanted to see one thing. They wanted to see Emmitt run.

He gave the fans a glimpse of the old Emmitt, running for 109 yards and breaking Payton's record on an 11-yard burst up the middle. Yeah, he probably would have broken it for a touchdown back in the day. But, back in the day, he normally didn't have a defender sniffing him for five yards.

The pomp and circumstance followed complete with a permanent banner in Texas Stadium. Jones and Smith had their mark.

They also had another Tony Dorsett situation on their hands. Jones went out and got himself the football man fans had clamored for 10 years when he brought former Giants, Patriots, and Jets coach Bill Parcells to town. Parcells took one look at the roster and wanted the Cowboys to get younger. He especially wanted them younger at running back.

Troy Hambrick had complained most of 2002 that he wasn't getting a chance and that Smith was retarding the Cowboys' progress. Probably true, but should Hambrick ever question Smith, even if Smith told him the sky was green?

Parcells thought so. He told Smith he was welcome to come back in a backup role, but that Hambrick was his starter. Smith's 975-yard performance the year before had snapped his streak of 11 consecutive 1,000-yard season. It now seemed his 13-year Dallas career was headed that way as well.

The Cowboys said goodbye to the franchise's greatest running back on March 27, 2003, when he signed with—Arizona? Tampa Bay, Baltimore, even a rival NFC East team would have been better. The Cardinals were, well, the Cardinals. They weren't even in the NFC East anymore.

The "E. SMITH" on the back of another jersey just looked so weird. Before he signed with Arizona, former "greatest running back in franchise history" Dorsett, who finished his career in Denver, warned Smith to protect his legacy. He told him not to make the same mistake.

In 2003, he returned to Dallas to a mixed reception. In the off-season, he told *Sports Illustrated* that in the last few years in Dallas he felt like "a diamond surrounded by trash." Smith said the quote was taken out of context, but Cowboys fans didn't really care in what context it was said. He got his boos; he got his cheers. He also got absolutely buried on his first carry for a five-yard loss. Remember Emmitt Smith for the warrior and legend he is.

His triumphant return to Texas Stadium was minus-one yard on six carries. The performance and the whole Cardinals experience should not be—and won't be—the way Smith is remembered.

Remember him as the top ground gainer in NFL history. Remember him for helping deliver three Super Bowls in four years to help the Cowboys become the team of the 1990s. Remember him for shredding the New York Giants with one arm barely attached to his shoulder.

LARRY
ALLEN

Larry Allen terrorized defensive linemen for 14 seasons. On this day, though, it was Allen's turn to be nervous. The soft-spoken offensive lineman from Compton, California, wiped sweat from his brow, took a deep breath and simply offered: "How about them Cowboys?"

For the next several minutes, the man who is widely considered the strongest person to play pro football displayed a vulnerable, tender side that never showed to opponents during his 12 seasons with the Cowboys and two with the San Francisco 49ers. When he finished, it was official: the behemoth lineman Dallas drafted in the second round of the 1994 NFL Draft from Sonoma State was a Pro Football Hall of Famer, joining Troy Aikman, Michael Irvin, and Emmitt Smith as Cowboys Hall of Famers in the Jerry Jones era.

During the speech, which Jones introduced, Allen said his daughter, Jayla Lee, had helped him write his remarks. Allen also asked for help from Cowboys fans on-hand, pleading for a "How about them Cowboys?" when he needed a hand.

On his way to 11 Pro Bowls and seven first-team all-pro selections, Allen rarely needed assistance. He made the NFL's all-decade team for the 1990s and 2000s, and is in the Cowboys' Ring of Honor. He also once bench pressed 705 pounds and squatted 905 pounds. He was also versatile, playing every offensive line position except center for the Cowboys at one point during his tenure. Of his seven all-pro selections, six came at guard and one at tackle. An impressive career for a wayward kid who didn't play football until he was a junior in high school.

For the mid-90s and early-00s Cowboys, Allen was a security blanket. Smith blasted through holes Allen created on his way to becoming the NFL's all-time leading rusher. Aikman and Irvin benefitted from the time—and comfort—Allen created. Allen played in 203 games and started all but six. He was durable, feared, and well-liked, all traits his mother, Vera, who raised Larry and his brother, Von, as a single parent, instilled in both of her boys.

ROUGH BEGINNINGS

Playing at 6-foot-3, 325 pounds, Allen was an imposing figure wherever he lined up. Things certainly didn't start that way. As an infant, Allen contracted meningitis and wasn't expected to live. While in junior high in an area of Los Angeles known for violent gangs, Allen was stabbed multiple times in a fight. Instead of being frightened, Allen's mother told him, as Allen said in his Hall of Fame speech, she "wasn't raising any punks." So, three months after being stabbed, Allen sought the perpetrator out and demanded a fight... and lost. On the second try, Allen lost again. The third

LARRY ALLEN

Born: November 27, 1971, in Los Angeles, California
Position: Guard/Tackle
Years with the Cowboys: 1994–2006
All-Pro/Pro Bowl Appearances: 7/11
Honors:
* Inducted into the Pro Football Hall of Fame in 2013
* Inducted into the Ring of Honor in 2011
* Ten Pro Bowl selections as a Cowboy, tied for second-most in team history behind Bob Lilly's 11.
* NFL All-Decade Team: 1990s
* NFL All-Decade Team: 2000s

attempt finally tilted things in Allen's favor. While he was fighting to defend himself and his brother, Allen said the incident taught him to never back down to anyone.

In addition to actual fights, Allen's family also fought the circumstance of their surroundings. Gang violence and related drug activity was a part of life. Consistently searching for an alternative path, especially after Von suffered a non-life-threatening gunshot wound, Vera moved the family often, leading to Allen attending multiple junior highs and high schools.

Before his senior year, Allen moved in with the family of Steve Hatton, with whom Allen had been close since the eighth grade. Living with the Hattons in Napa, California, Allen moved from defense to offense and played his senior year at Vintage High School.

Though Allen didn't graduate high school, he enrolled at Butte College in Oroville, California, after Butte coach Craig Rigsbee guided Allen to a GED and enough academic credits to enroll. From Butte, though, Allen returned to Compton, again without finishing a degree plan. Sonoma State coach Frank Scalercio had seen Allen at Butte, but thought Allen would have other offers. Instead, Scalercio found Allen in Compton and persuaded him to get his academics to a point he could be accepted into school. Relying on an area adult school, Allen did finish his degree and did end up at Sonoma State, where he dominated.

LINING IT UP

During his two years, Allen gave up one sack and made the Division II All-America team both years. He also played in the Senior Bowl and the East-West Shrine Game, two games that cemented what the Cowboys knew: Larry Allen not only could play in the NFL, but Larry Allen could be an NFL star.

When he was drafted with the 46th pick in the 1994 NFL Draft, Allen became the first Sonoma State player ever drafted. He was also the 10th offensive lineman selected that year. The Cowboys hadn't taken an offensive lineman as high as the second round since 1981. Allen was on only one of the Cowboys' three Super Bowl teams in the '90s and he never played for Jimmy Johnson. Four games into his rookie year, Mark Tuinei went down with an injured back. Allen started his first NFL game in Tuinei's place, and was a permanent fixture just weeks later. The next season, Allen earned his first trip to the Pro Bowl, receiving the honor alongside four other Cowboys offensive lineman. For the next decade, No. 73 was a consistent presence coming out of the Dallas huddle. Versatile and athletic, Allen was also fairly durable for his position. In 2005, his 11th season, he played every snap and made his 10th Pro Bowl.

In 2006, the Cowboys released Allen, who promptly signed with San Francisco. That year, he made the Pro Bowl for a final time and helped Frank Gore rush for 1,695 yards. Even in his final season, Allen started every game for the 49ers.

In retirement, Allen keeps up with his three grown children. He may also be attending more NFL games soon. Allen's son, Larry Allen III, is an all-Ivy League offensive lineman at Harvard and majoring in biomedical engineering.

The elder Allen has given his children a childhood far different from the one he experienced. However, the tribulations, the challenges, the difficulties, the bumps, the bruises, the setbacks Allen endured went into chiseling a foundation that led to February 2, 2013, in Canton, Ohio. On that day, Allen stepped up to a podium anxious and nervous. And, as likely the greatest offensive lineman in history, took his rightful place in the Pro Football Hall of Fame.

AP PHOTO/MICHAEL AINSWORTH

JERRY
JONES

On the surface, Jerry Jones has it all. He has owned one of the most valuable sports properties in the world for almost 30 years, a business that intricately involves his three children and is a true family affair. He is part of the 2017 Pro Football Hall of Fame class, and has seen four others (Emmitt Smith, Troy Aikman, Michael Irvin, and Larry Allen) inducted who played for his Cowboys.

Amongst NFL owners, he is considered one of the league's best and most creative, consistently trying to find ways to expand the game and its revenues. Jones continues to be successful outside football with his oil and gas ventures—the industry that, well, fueled his purchase of the Cowboys in 1989—and his real estate investments, which include the franchise's sparkling The Star complex in Frisco, a suburb north of Dallas. The team's AT&T Stadium is a draw itself that has hosted almost every big American sporting event. Jones's watch includes three Super Bowl championships. Players like playing for him. And fans still come from all over to see a franchise that is truly a global brand. Jones is also charitable, personal, even accessible. He is a master of homespun witticisms and run-on sentences.

Yes, on the surface, the self-made Arkansas billionaire is the kind of heart-of-America narrative that should be easy to like . . . on the surface.

But, as Jones has readily admitted, he wants more, something that Jones the businessman, the NFL owner, the altruist, the controversial public figure, can't simply purchase or "good business" his way to getting: another Super Bowl trophy. One truly won his way.

It's at this intersection of Jones' burning desire to hold the Lombardi Trophy again and his other job in the organization that has resulted in a maddening relationship with Cowboys fans, and has led to sharp, stinging criticisms from pundits. For, while Jerry Jones the owner is an innovator and a true Hall of Famer, Jerry Jones the General Manager has presided over one of the most middling NFL franchises for over 20 years.

In this role is where Jones made a decision that long-time Cowboys fans have not forgotten and one that fans the flames of Jones's below-the-surface, competitive flames: he fired Jimmy Johnson, his former college roommate, the coach he hired minutes after buying the team, the coach who won two Super Bowls, built the team that won the third, and made the Cowboys the Cowboys again. And, while even Jones admits he should have had more patience before handing Johnson a $2 million check and waving goodbye, this March 1994 decision has, to most Cowboys fans, defined the Jerry Jones era.

Johnson was the coach who made fans, somewhat, forget how Jones quickly and, to some, brashly fired the legendary gentleman coach Tom Landry. Johnson brought America's Team back with the same swagger, style, and success he had at the University of Miami. And it was Jones who gave Johnson to Cowboys fans. It was also Jones who took him away.

JERRY JONES

Born: October 13, 1942, in Inglewood, California
Position: Owner, President, General Manager
Years with the Cowboys: 1989–Present
Career Highlights:
* Super Bowl Champions: XXVII, XXVIII, XXX
* Considered one of the NFL's most powerful, controversial, and innovative owners
* Four of Jones' players have been inducted into the Pro Football Hall of Fame (Emmitt Smith, Troy Aikman, Michael Irvin, Larry Allen)
* Twenty-two different Jones players have made at least one All-Pro team
* At an estimated $4 billion, owns one of the world's most valuable sports franchises.
Honors:
* Inducted into the Pro Football Hall of Fame in 2017
* 2014 NFL Executive of the Year

The convenient explanation is that Jones wanted more credit for the two Super Bowls, that Jones wanted to be known as a "football guy." Jones has long maintained the answer is more complex, that the relationship between him and Johnson was more complicated than it appeared publicly. Jones also insists football decisions that involved money did go through him. And, while the Cowboys did win another Super Bowl in 1996 with Barry Switzer on the sidelines, that title is still seen as a championship won with "Jimmy's players."

So, until that lingering flame is extinguished with a smiling Jones holding yet another Super Bowl trophy, one accomplished without Johnson's still-looming shadow, the desire to make his team better, the league better, the game better, more popular, more profitable is going to be there. Just as it always has been, even if has been lingering just below the surface of the Jerry Jones veneer.

BROYLES' BOYS BECOME COWBOYS

Jones is often criticized for inserting himself too frequently into "football decisions." However, among NFL owners, the Carolina Panthers' Jerry Richardson being another, Jones has a legitimate football background. As a fullback-turned-offensive-lineman, Jones played for legendary Arkansas Razorbacks coach Frank Broyles. Known as an innovator and one of the sharpest football minds of his day, Broyles also surrounded himself with keen minds. When Jones played at Arkansas, Switzer, Hayden Fry, later a legend at Iowa, and former Tennessee and Pittsburgh coach Johnny Majors were all of the staff. The Hogs won a national title, and, most importantly for his future position, Jones met a Port Arthur, Texas, native who happened to be paired with him on road trips: Jimmy Johnson.

Jones arrived at Arkansas having already learned to be a salesman. His father, Pat, owned a grocery store where Jerry would stock shelves and interact with customers. These interactions and listening to how his father talked to customers and elicited promises of repeat business are the roots of Jones' easy conversational ways and his ease of being around different people.

Jones married his Arkansas sweetheart, Gene, his sophomore year of college, the same year he read a "Life" magazine article on Cleveland Browns owner Art Modell while on an Arkansas football road trip. After graduating from college, Jones, at 23 years old, scraped up enough investors and lines of credit to actually try to buy the Los Angeles Chargers from the hotel icon Barron Hilton. Jones's dad, concerned about the massive debt that his son would be tied to, talked Jones out of the deal.

Instead, Jones started an oil and gas company that, at first, had little success. These hardships produced a story Jones enjoys now telling about how he was in such debt that a rental car agent at a counter at Dallas Love Field airport actually cut up his credit card in front of him.

Still, Jones was not deterred. Instead, he pressed on with the same unbridled enthusiasm he still exudes. And, it wasn't long until success followed. The wildcatting Jones hit a succession of oil wells that soon had him thinking about getting back into the football business. When then-Cowboys owner Bum Bright announced he was selling the Cowboys, Jones made a call, even though he knew Bright did not know him or if he would even take Jones seriously.

Bright did takes Jones seriously, and the two men shook hands on a deal in early February 1989 to sell the team to Jones for $151 million. The next morning, Bright called Jones back and said another group had just offered $10 million more and that Jones could simply sell the team to them and make a nice profit.

Jones turned the deal down, choosing, instead, to hire Johnson from Miami, and start building a football team.

INNOVATOR, VISIONARY

Turning down the quick $10 million profit to sell the Cowboys the morning after agreeing to buy the franchise was, in short, a good one. The franchise is now worth, according to Forbes' 2015 numbers, $4 billion, making the Cowboys the world's most valuable sports brand. And, while Jones has taken a large amount of biting criticism for his general manager duties, there is no doubting Jones' impact on the NFL's business. The franchise has a unique merchandise distribution agreement, and a long-term sponsorship deal with AT&T. The Cowboys continue to be a global brand and have long been the most popular NFL team in Mexico.

In 2016, the team made the move from its long-time headquarters in Valley Ranch in a suburb west of Dallas to the sprawling northern suburb of Frisco and its new home, The Star. Jones started investing in parcels of land around the city years ago, anticipating substantial growth in the area. Now, with The Star as a major centerpiece, Frisco and The Star have also become a destination with a world-class practice facility and an area to host varied events.

At Jones' main facility, AT&T Stadium, he has welcomed concerts, the Final Four, NBA All-Star weekend, the Super Bowl, WrestleMania, the College Football Playoff, and many other college and high school football events. In short, the Cowboys have become a brand that extends beyond football, just like its iconic owner.

Until that next Super Bowl comes, Jones will press forward, spreading himself as thin as ever and receiving as much criticism as ever. Some will be valid, some will be humorous, some beneficial, some will hurt. But, they won't deter Jones's focus on making his franchise better, the league he's a part of more successful. They also won't hold him back from chasing down the last ghost, that one title that will bring Jerry Jones, the owner, the general manager, the visionary, the innovator, the businessman, to finally, in his mind, have it all.

TEXAS STADIUM

Even in the face of destruction, Texas Stadium held firm. The venerable structure at the intersection of Highways 114 and 183 in Irving that housed Doomsday, Landry, the Triplets, and America's Team was going quickly, but not easily or quietly.

It was April 11, 2010, more than a year after the stadium's most famous tenant moved west to Arlington and to its new $1.2 billion house with the massive video board. One push from an 11-year-old essay contest winner and 30 seconds later, Texas Stadium would be reduced to memories and a rubble pile. When Casey Rogers began the process, smoke billowed, the ground shook, and the stadium with the turf Walt Garrison once called "harder than Chinese arithmetic" completely crumbled.

Well, almost. On the far side of the grounds the Texas Department of Transportation would shortly take over and convert to a construction staging area, three pillars bent, but didn't fall, a last act of defiance from a place that opened in 1971 as the zenith of NFL stadiums and that introduced the league to some of its most important on- and off-field innovations. From concerts, revivals, wrestling matches, and motocross races to high school state title games, the Big 12 Championship game, NFC Championship Games, and even the Pro Bowl, Texas Stadium ushered in a new stadium standard, from its cost to its quirky characteristics to being the stage for Tex Schramm's and Tom Landry's creative visions.

Perhaps it was fitting that the three beams remained, as it was a structural integrity question raised during construction that led to Texas Stadium's unique, partially-covered roof, a feature that made the stadium a ubiquitous, recognizable symbol of the team, city, and state. The original plan called for an enclosed stadium. However, after completing only a small part of the effort, engineers concluded the structurally independent roof could not handle the extra weight. So, while those watching would be covered, the playing surface would not. Originally thought to be a failure, the "flaw" brought significant attention to both the stadium and the team, especially as an opening credits mainstay from 1978–91 on the worldwide television hit, *Dallas*.

D.D. Lewis, a popular linebacker from the '70s teams, famously quipped that the hole was there "so God could watch his favorite football team play." If so, the divine took a winding path of happy accidents to get from the Cotton

Bowl in Dallas' Fair Park to a sleepy western suburb. For its first 11-plus seasons, the Cowboys played in the stadium just east of downtown better known for its annual college bowl game (also now played in Cowboys Stadium). In the mid-'60s, however, owner Clint Murchison began to worry that the area around the Cotton Bowl had grown unattractive to his ticket-buying base. He approached Dallas mayor J. Erik Jonsson about putting a new stadium proposal before city voters as part of a civic bond package. Jonsson declined Murchison's request and refused to put the measure on a ballot. So, after giving Jonsson multiple opportunities to relent, Murchison and Schramm announced in late 1967 they had signed an agreement with the City of Irving to build Texas Stadium.

Costing $35 million (approximately $200 million in 2013) and featuring 381 luxury suites, Texas Stadium was a marvel as much for its ambition as its audacity. Fans were required to pay for the right to buy tickets and those wanting to sit in one of the luxury suites, then called the Circle Suites, paid as much as an absurd $50,000 for the right. Some players complained about a Roman Coliseum-like atmosphere in which the wine-sipping, aristocratic oil barons and baronesses watched in covered comfort as relatively low-paid players entertained them on the stadium's notoriously hard surface and crowned field.

Players eventually grew to enjoy the nuances of their suburban home. After playing two games at the Cotton Bowl to open the 1971 season, the Cowboys made good on their promise to leave Dallas proper, christening their new home with the Astroturf field on October 24, beating New England, 44–21, behind two Roger Staubach touchdown passes and Duane Thomas' 56-yard run. Dallas won its first 10 games in the new stadium, won the first of five Super Bowls in the building's inaugural campaign, and didn't have a losing season while calling Texas Stadium home until 1986.

The stadium also expanded the idea that other events could be successful in football stadiums. While others had held a handful of events, Texas Stadium focused on being a destination venue for other entertainment forms. In addition to being the home of Craig James, Eric Dickerson, and the rest of the SMU Mustangs from 1979–86, major entities of all stripes used the stadium. Texas Stadium also became a marquee venue for Texas high school football games in all classifications, giving generations of Texas schoolboys the opportunity to play on the same surface as their heroes.

In its later years, Texas Stadium fell into disrepair. The City of Irving finally repainted the roof in 2006, the first time it had been repainted since its original finish in 1971. By then, Jerry Jones had announced he was leaving for Arlington and yet another stadium that would set the standard.

During its 37 years, Texas Stadium was the Dallas Cowboys' stage. The Dallas Cowboys became the Dallas Cowboys there. History happened there. Moments happened there. Below is a look at the Top 10 Texas Stadium moments/impacts:

10. Non-football events: In September 1971, Texas Stadium opened its doors with a 10-day revival from noted pastor Billy Graham. Johnny and June Cash performed and future President and First Lady Laura and George W. Bush attended. The event was simply the first of a litany of major events. In 1972 and then from 1984–88, Dallas-based World Class Championship Wrestling, featuring the legendary Von Erich family, held its annual "Parade of Champions" shows at Texas Stadium. The most famous match happened on May 6, 1984, when Kerry Von Erich beat "Nature Boy" Ric Flair for the NWA title in front of over 50,000 fans, only months after Kerry's brother, David Von Erich, died in Tokyo. On the music side, the Jackson Five, Paul McCartney, Elton John, Metallica, Alabama, and Madonna all played at Texas Stadium. In 1993, country star Garth Brooks filmed a live concert at the stadium for an NBC special. In addition to simulating a thunderstorm, Brooks had special bars installed that allowed him to, in essence, zip line from the stage to various parts of the stadium. The "Garth Bars" became a permanent fixture.

Texas Stadium also hosted one of the most famous high school football games, a 1994 playoff game between John Tyler and Plano East that John Tyler won 48–44. The game is known for Plano East recovering three onside kicks in the final moments only to see John Tyler return a long kickoff for a touchdown with three seconds left to win the game. The anguish in the Plano East call went viral and earned that day's broadcasting trio, Eddy Clinton, Denny Garver, and Mike Zoffuto, acclaim.

9. Jason Garrett's second-half comeback vs. Green Bay on Thanksgiving Day 1994: Before he became the Cowboys head coach, Jason

Garrett was a clipboard-carrying, Princeton-educated, third-stringer looking up at Troy Aikman and Rodney Peete. The Sunday before the annual Thanksgiving game at Texas Stadium, both Aikman and Peete were hurt in a win over the Redskins. Garrett actually threw five passes against Washington, but knew the real test would come at home four days later against an aggressive Packers defense. Things did not start well. Terrell Buckley intercepted Garrett's first pass and Green Bay led 17–6 at the half. Then, things did go well. In less than 20 minutes, Garrett led the Cowboys on five touchdown drives and to a franchise-record 36 second-half points in a 42–31 win. Peete returned the next week, Aikman the week after, and the Cowboys eventually lost to San Francisco in the NFC Championship Game.

8. George Teague/Terrell Owens, Sept. 24, 2000: After hauling in a 3-yard second-quarter touchdown pass, San Francisco 49ers wide receiver Terrell Owens raced to the blue star that graced midfield at Texas Stadium and celebrated his achievement. Not amused, Cowboys running back Emmitt Smith did the same after a 1-yard plunge shortly thereafter. In the fourth quarter, Owens scored again to put the 49ers ahead 41–17. And, again, he raced to midfield to mark his efforts. Dallas safety George Teague made sure he had company, knocking Owens down and starting as much of a melee as can be started in a 24-point route. Teague's career ended a year later. Owens later signed with Dallas and was an All-Pro for the franchise in 2007.

7. Leon Lett's misfire vs. Miami, Thanksgiving Day 1993: Confusion was abundant when Miami visited Texas Stadium on Thanksgiving Day 1993. A rare November North Texas snowstorm blanketed the field and paralyzed both offenses. In the waning moments and with Dallas clinging to a 14–13 lead, Jimmie Jones blocked Pete Stoyanovich's 47-yard field goal try. The ball came to rest close to the goal line with 10 Cowboys players standing far away, waving their arms to let teammates know to stay away. Leon Lett did not get the message. Instead, the defensive tackle that piled up 22.5 sacks in 10 years with Dallas, jumped between three Dolphins and tried to recover the ball. The attempt failed, the ball squirted loose, Miami recovered, and Stoyanovich nailed a 19-yard field goal with three seconds left to give the Dolphins the win. The moment is memorable, but fairly inconsequential, as Dallas didn't lose again on its way to a 12–4 season and a Super Bowl win over Buffalo.

6. Clint Longley's comeback vs. Washington, Thanksgiving Day 1974:
Nicknamed "The Mad Bomber" because he often clanked throws in practice off Tom Landry's famous coaching tower, the Abilene Christian product got it right for a few moments against the Redskins on Thanksgiving Day 1974. Trailing 16–3 in the third quarter, Longley joined the huddle after Washington knocked Roger Staubach out with a concussion. He quickly hit Billy Joe DuPree for a 35-yard touchdown to cut the lead to six points. After trading touchdowns, Longley found Drew Pearson for a 50-yard score with 35 seconds left and the win. Though exciting, the game meant little. Dallas went 8–6 that year, ending a string of eight straight playoff appearances. Two years later, Longley punched Staubach in training camp, and was subsequently traded and out of football after playing three games for San Diego in 1976.

5. Captain Comeback's Last Ride, December 16, 1979: In a career filled with stirring, last-moment heroics, quarterback Roger Staubach's 21st and final Cowboys comeback may have been his most thrilling. After trading punches, Staubach found Ron Springs for a 26-yard fourth quarter touchdown pass. On the next drive, Larry Cole met Redskins running back John Riggins in the gap on third down and prevented Washington from extending its 34–28 lead. That gave Captain Comeback a chance, an opportunity Staubach capitalized on by hitting Tony Hill from eight yards out with 39 seconds to give the Cowboys a 35–34 win in a game Staubach called in his book *Hail Mary* "the most thrilling 60 minutes I ever spent on a football field." A week later, Staubach played his last game, a 21–19 loss to the Los Angeles Rams at Texas Stadium.

4. Original Personal Seat Licenses/Stadium Sponsorships: Texas Stadium is often credited with being the first of a new generation of NFL stadiums. It also laid the foundation for the revenue-generating machine the league is now. When it opened in 1971, then-owner Clint Murchison required season-ticket holders to buy bonds to guarantee their rights to buy tickets, the precursor to the personal seat license requirements most teams now have in place. Also, in the mid-'90s, current Cowboys owner Jerry Jones went outside the standard NFL corporate sponsorship agreements and signed deals with Pepsi and Nike to become the official Texas Stadium sponsors. The NFL sued Jones, and Jones countersued. The two eventually dropped the suits and the franchise maintained the sponsorships. Jones still outpaces his competitors in this arena, generating $80 million in independent sponsorship for Cowboys Stadium in 2012, about four times more than any other team.

3. Saying goodbye, December 20, 2008: The last game at Texas Stadium is notable for what it ushered in and for what the opponent did. Down 19–17, Baltimore's Willis McGahee scampered 77 yards for a touchdown to give the Ravens a 26–17 lead. The run tied for the longest ever by an opponent, a mark Le'Ron McClain broke on Baltimore's next offensive snap with an 82-yard dash to seal a 33–24 win. Not long after, the Cowboys said goodbye to a stadium that once set the standard for NFL stadiums in favor of one likely to do the same for those in the near future. Nine months after losing to the Ravens in the final Texas Stadium game, Dallas opened Cowboys Stadium in Arlington in front of 105,000 and a national television audience with a 33–31 loss to the New York Giants. Inside the new $1.2 billion palace, fans were treated to a video board that weighs 1.2 million pounds, is equivalent to 5,000 52' flat panel televisions and cost $40 million. Dallas finished the season 12–6 and won its first playoff game since 1996. Less than 16 months after hosting its final game, Texas Stadium came down in a controlled demolition.

2. Emmitt's record run, October 27, 2002: After leading the Cowboys to the 1992 Super Bowl title with a league-leading 1,713 yards and 18 touchdowns, Emmitt Smith and Jerry Jones were at odds. Jones didn't want to give a big contract to a running back that led the league with 365 carries in 1991 and who had 373 in 1992. Smith said little and held out for a new deal. When the Cowboys started 0–2 in 1993, he got one. A week later, Smith, who still led the league in rushing despite the two-week absence, was in the lineup, the Cowboys won another Super Bowl, and Smith didn't come out of the Dallas backfield for almost 10 more years. Smith capped his Cowboys career in 2002 when, against Seattle, he took a handoff from Chad Hutchinson and, with an 11-yard run, broke Walter Payton's all-time rushing record. The Hall of Famer left the Cowboys after the season and played two final seasons with Arizona, finishing with 18,355 yards, just over 1,600 more than Payton.

1. Jimmy's guarantee, January 23, 1994: Jimmy Johnson normally makes things clear. On the Thursday before the Cowboys–49ers 1993 NFC Championship Game, Johnson ensured those listening to Randy Galloway's local radio show learned a little about newspaper terminology and the

Cowboys head coach's hubris. Driving home from practice, Johnson called Galloway's show and guaranteed Dallas would be going to the Super Bowl. "You can put it in 3-inch headlines. We will win the ballgame." The *Dallas Morning News* put the guarantee in half-inch type, but gave the proclamation front-page billing, next to a headline concerning Whitewater and the Clintons. That disappointed Johnson, who added, "we would have gotten 3-inch headlines if the story had been on the sports page." No one in San Francisco had a hard time finding the comments. "The man's got balls," 49ers coach George Seifert said in reaction. "I don't know if they're brass or paper-mache. We'll find out soon." Less than two days later, everyone found out. Dallas raced to a 28–7 halftime lead on its way to a 38–21 victory and its second consecutive Super Bowl title. The game turned out to be Johnson's last in Texas Stadium. He parted ways with Jones and the Cowboys two months after the Super Bowl win over Buffalo. Dallas won the Super Bowl again under Barry Switzer two years later and made the playoffs in 1996, but has only two playoff wins since.